Working Horses

The Farmer's Market
— H.H. Bennett Studio

Working Horses

Looking Back 100 Years
to America's Horse-Drawn Days

— With 300 Historic Photographs —

Charles Philip Fox

Heart Prairie Press
P.O. Box 332
Whitewater, Wisconsin 53190

Reprinted 1991

Printed in the United States of America

Page Layout and Design by Joseph Mischka

Published by
Heart Prairie Press
Box 322
Whitewater, WI 53190

Publisher's Cataloging in Publication Data

Fox, Charles Philip, 1913-
    Working horses : looking back 100 years to America's horse-drawn days / Charles Philip Fox. --
    p. cm.
    Includes bibliographical references and index.
    ISBN 0-9622663-2-9

    1.Draft horses--United States--History. 2. Horse-drawn vehicles --United States--History. 3. Draft horses--United States--Pictorial works. 4. Horse-drawn vehicles--United States--Pictorial works.
I. Title.

SF311.3.U6   636.1'5'0973
                                  QBI90-90
                                      MARC

Contents

Dedication

to

Dick and Joy Sparrow

inspiring friends for 30 years.

Dick Sparrow driving his 40-horse-hitch for Schlitz Brewing Co. in the 1973 Great Circus Parade in Milwaukee

Introduction

Working Horses

**When horsepower really meant
'horse power,' these animals did it all.**

It is difficult to believe that man was completely dependent on horses — to move freight; build roads; deliver milk, ice and coal; gallop over city streets with huge pieces of fire equipment; pull ambulances; deliver mail; move circuses; haul street cars and to do any other work that needed to be done.

Yet a century ago this was the normal state of affairs.

For those who love, enjoy or own horses, whether draft or riding, this book is designed to be a pleasurable experience to pick up and open to any page.

Reminiscing with these nostalgic photographs and prints will make any horseman or horsewoman appreciate the significance of the workhorse in the development of America.

Charles Philip Fox

Acknowledgments

In the process of compiling these photographs I have received exceptional cooperation from this group of people which I am pleased to acknowledge.

Philip Weber, Cleveland, Ohio

Norm Coughlin, Chicago, Ill.

Anna Fox, Oregon, Wis.

Bill Noonan, North Weymouth, Mass.

Gene Baxter, Troy, N.Y.

Robert Mischka, Whitewater, Wis.

Jim Richendollar, Belleville, Mich.

Dr. H.J. McGinnis, Waupaca, Wis.

Ron Ryder, Boonville, N.Y.

Robert Chandler, San Fransisco, Calif.

Wesley Jung, Sheboygan, Wis.

Buckley's lunch wagons were generally 16-feet long, 7-feet wide and 10-feet high. The craftsmanship displayed in their construction was superb.

— *E.B. Luce Corp.*

Chapter One

Building the Vehicles

Almost every town of any size had a wagon and carriage builder. These craftsmen only built the special bodies wanted by their local customers. There were other sources for springs, wheels, special hardware, axles and even complete undercarriages. This simplified the construction of vehicles. With the onset of motorcars and trucks, it was inevitable that the production of horse drawn vehicles would subside.

For example, the U.S. Census Bureau reported that in 1890, there were 80 carriage companies in Cincinnati, Ohio, that employed 9,000 workers who produced 130,000 vehicles. By 1911, there were only 32 such companies left in the city.

Of course, there were the very large manufacturers. Studebaker in South Bend, Indiana, produced 75,000 horse drawn vehicles a year. Kentucky Wagon Mfg. Co. in Louisville had a yearly production of 90,000 wagons.

The big mail order houses did a tremendous business on carriages selling from $25 to $60. The body was generally crated and shipped with the wheels removed.

Many wagon builders developed specialized vehicles required by commerce. Examples of these were funeral hearses that were extra fancy in design, or wagons designed just for the breweries.

Abbot, Downing & Co. of Concord, New Hampshire, was so successful in building a durable stage coach that their product became known as the Concord Coach. This company also offered a complete line of other horse drawn vehicles.

Firefighting equipment was very specialized and, generally speaking, the companies that produced these complicated vehicles did not produce other vehicles. There were exceptions. The Jung Carriage Company in Sheboygan, Wisconsin, manufactured a few hose carts, but these were not much different than solid delivery wagons with a few added requirements such as running boards for men, full rear steps, bell, heavier wheels. These carts, of course, were painted bright red.

The big railroad circuses found few wagon builders that could produce the massive and rugged wagons which they needed to survive under the severe, daily conditions of their industry. The loads were enormous and the wagons had to hold up regardless of conditions at the show grounds. Rainy days produced muddy lots. The grounds might be sandy or rock-strewn. The show went on in a different town almost every day.

As the motor age chugged into existence in the first 20 years of the 20th century, wagon manufacturers went out of business. Circuses then hired their own wagon builders. The big draft horses did not leave the circus scene until the late 1930s. Many of the circus wagonmasters of this era were geniuses in producing superb equipment.

Interior view of the Abbot-Downing factory about 1880. Abbot-Downing Co. produced a varied line of horse drawn vehicles.

It was in 1826 that Abbot joined Downing in his Concord, NH, shop. These men developed the coach that became the standard for western travel.

Abbot and Downing broke up their partnership in 1847 and each went their separate ways. In 1865, the two companies merged again. Whether alone or separate, their vehicles were of the highest quality.

— *New Hampshire Historical Society*

Opposite: Biddle & Smart Co. advertise over 176 styles of vehicles. It is difficult to comprehend the need for such a variety of conveyances. 1890.

— *Author's Collection*

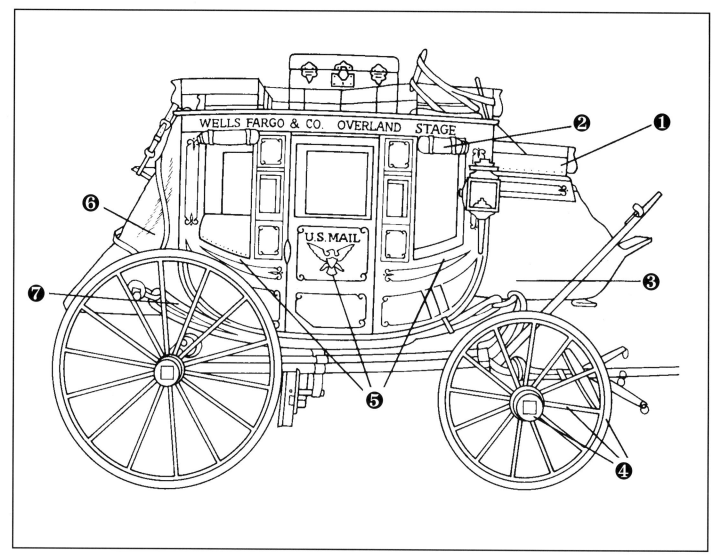

❶ Driver's Box — The celebrated stagecoach driver negotiated precarious, rocky trails requiring a cool head and complete command of coach and team.

❷ Curtains — Rolled down for protection of passengers against rain, mud, dust and cold weather, curtains were made of leather or canvas.

❸ Front Boot — Leather baggage compartment under driver's seat in which the famous Wells Fargo Treasure Box was carried for safekeeping.

❹ Wheel — The hub was made of seasoned elm with spokes of tough oak and an iron rim.

❺ Coach Body Panels — A special skill of the coachmaker was the steaming and curving of basswood panels to fit the durable ash frame of the coach body.

❻ Rear Boot — Leather storage compartment, larger than the front boot, consisting of a platform hinged to the coach and supported by two chains.

❼ Thoroughbrace — Multi-layered leather straps of thick steerhide which supported the coach body, one on each side, and functioned as shock absorbers.

AN EXPRESS FREIGHT SHIPMENT OF 30 COACHES, APRIL 15, 1868
BY ABBOT, DOWNING & CO., CONCORD, N.H. TO WELLS, FARGO CO., OMAHA, NEB.

Above: In the 1860's, Wells Fargo owned and operated the most extensive stage coach system in the west. They settled on the Concord Coach as their standard equipment. (The Bank today uses this vehicle as a corporate symbol.)

In 1867, Wells Fargo ordered 40 of the coaches. The red painted bodies ornamented with gold scrolls and a landscape painted on the doors and straw-colored wheels were quite elegant as they flashed in and out of towns and stage stops between.

The photo is of a painting produced by John Burgum, the artist who painted the landscapes on the coach doors.

His rendition shows a shipment of 30 coaches of the huge order leaving the Abbot-Downing factory April 15, 1868, enroute to Wells Fargo Co. in Omaha, Neb.

— *New Hampshire Historical Society*

Opposite: In the horse drawn era, there was one vehicle that stood out and was identifiable — the Concord Stagecoach.

The entire vehicle was well-built to withstand the pounding it received daily on rough roads behind a team of four or six galloping horses.

The suspension system provided a more comfortable swinging motion. Mark Twain described the Concord Coach as "an imposing cradle on wheels."

It was a good-looking rig with a curved body rather than the boxy shape of other models. It acquired its name from the town where it was manufactured, Concord, NH., the home of the builders Abbot-Downing.

— *Wells Fargo Bank History Room*

T.H. Buckley of Worcester, Mass., was probably the lunch wagon king. In 1888, he built his first wagon as a place to sell his famous oyster stew. He soon realized it would be more profitable to build and sell lunch wagons than sell stew. By 1898, the T.H. Buckley Lunch Wagon Mfg. Co. was flourishing. He had these horse drawn restaurants located in over 275 cities.

This view of the interior of his shop shows the body frame under construction. The photo also gives a hint of other aspects of his output, namely specialized work done on the interior of railroad cars for travelling shows — in this case, Downies Big Uncle Tom's Cabin production.

— E.B. Luce Corp.

Left: The interior of Murphy's Cafe is slick, clean and well finished. The label on the door states "Worcester Lunch Car Mfg. Co. 1906 Worcester, Mass."

— *E.B. Luce Corp.*

Below: The beauty of Buckley's finished product was startling. This was important as no matter where the owner parked his restaurant, the vehicle was attractive and not an eyesore. His artist, C.K.Hardy,embellished the generally white vehicles with beautiful scrolls, designs and lettering. The initials A.E.C. refer to American Eagle Cafe, a name Buckley used. Note the etched glass panels. The left hand panel announces "Sandwiches, Pies, Coffee, Milk and Cigars.

— *E.B. Luce Corp.*

Beggs Wagon Co.

MANUFACTURERS OF

CIRCUS WAGONS

Band Wagons, Ticket Wagons, Cages, Calliopes, Racing Chariots,
Tableau Wagons, Baggage Wagons, Carnival Wagons,
Gears and Wagon Parts

35—YEARS EXPERIENCE—35

—— OFFICE AND FACTORY ——
MICHIGAN AND GUINOTTE AVENUES   **Kansas City, Mo., U. S. A.**

Wood Carved
and
Gilded

Or
Paint Pictures,
Gold and Paint
Scrolls

Made "A Little Better Than Seems Necessary"

Parade Wagons

AS FINE AS CAN BE PRODUCED

There is No Limit to Our Ability to Furnish any Style or Size Wanted

Give us your ideas and we will forward specifications and price.

2

Air Calliope

An Air Calliope that is a Real Musical Instrument

These Calliopes can be toned to accompany band or orchestra, or made VERY LOUD for parade.

The whistles and keyboard are made by the Tangley Mfg. Co. and are guaranteed by them for one year.

Three Sizes:

To load in baggage cars—
1,300 lbs.

For Wagon Shows—
1,600 lbs.

For Railroad Shows—
2,000 to 3,000 lbs.

We furnish them complete with gasoline engine and blower installed ready for use.

5

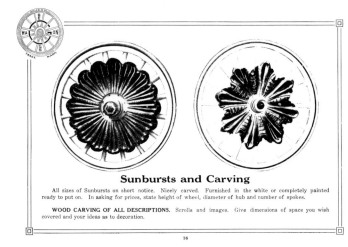

Sunbursts and Carving

All sizes of Sunbursts on short notice. Nicely carved. Furnished in the white or completely painted ready to put on. In asking for prices, state height of wheel, diameter of hub and number of spokes.

WOOD CARVING OF ALL DESCRIPTIONS. Scrolls and images. Give dimensions of space you wish covered and your ideas as to decoration.

16

WE MAKE

CAGES

All Sizes,

Wood Carved and Gilded

or Paint and Gold Scrolled.

Dens open one or two sides.

Give us your ideas and our estimates will be forwarded with price.

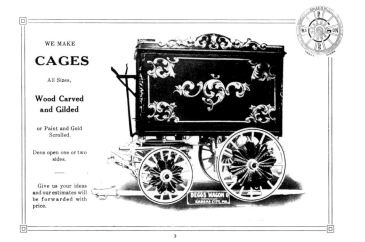

3

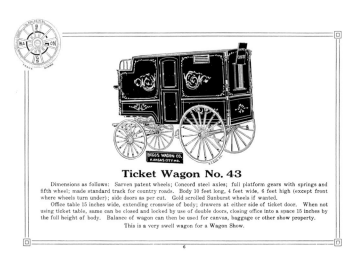

Ticket Wagon No. 43

Dimensions as follows: Sarven patent wheels; Concord steel axles; full platform gears with springs and fifth wheel; made standard track for country roads. Body 10 feet long, 4 feet wide, 6 feet high (except front where wheels turn under); side doors as per cut. Gold scrolled Sunburst wheels if wanted.

Office table 15 inches wide, extending crosswise of body; drawers at either side of ticket door. When not using ticket table, same can be closed and locked by use of double doors, closing office into a space 15 inches by the full height of body. Balance of wagon can then be used for canvas, baggage or other show property.

This is a very swell wagon for a Wagon Show.

6

The interesting fact about circus wagons is that they are all unique — there are no two alike — each was built to haul a specific load.

In 1910, the Beggs Wagon Co. had a special catalogue illustrating some examples of their products.

The Beggs letterhead had this slogan: "Made a little better than seems necessary."

— *Author's Collection*

Left: In 1908, the Columbus Carriage & Harness Co. ran this advertisement in the Breeder's Gazette. The small ad below for the U.S. Buggy & Cart Co. brags they have 150 styles of vehicles to choose from.

— *Author's Collection*

Below: One of the few horse drawn vehicle manufacturers that successfully made the transition to automobiles was Studebaker.

This advertisement appeared in a 1909 Bit & Spur magazine and it points out that "each Studebaker vehicle (is) a masterpiece of the carriage builder's art."

— *Anna Fox Collection*

Today, the Fruehauf Company manufacturers semitrailers. In their early days, they produced fine horse drawn equipment.

— *Philip Weber Collection*

Wheels of all sizes or wheel parts such as spokes, hubs and felloes were available. This 1860 ad offers wagon manufacturers these products.

— *Author's Collection*

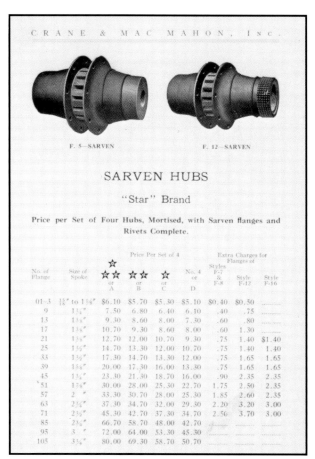

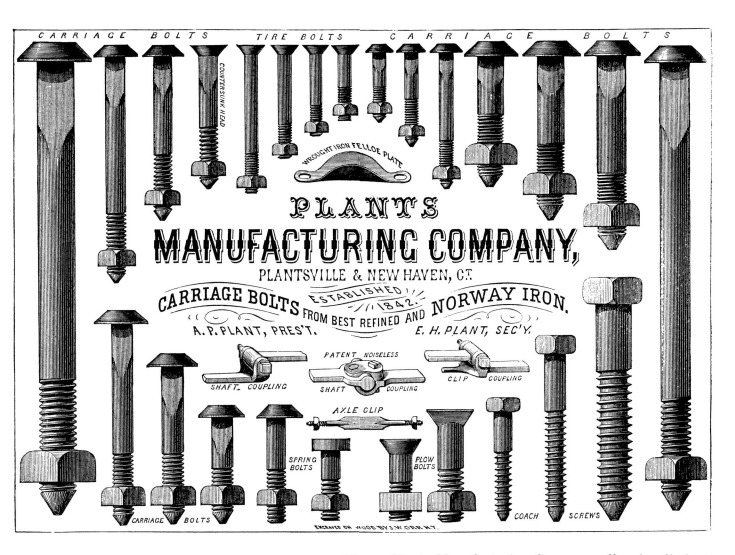

Above: Plants Manufacturing Company offered a distinct line of specialty bolts for carriage and wagon producers. 1860.

— Author's Collection

Opposite: These pages are from a 1925 catalogue of the St. Mary's Wheel & Spoke Co. in St. Mary's, Ohio.

— Author's Collection

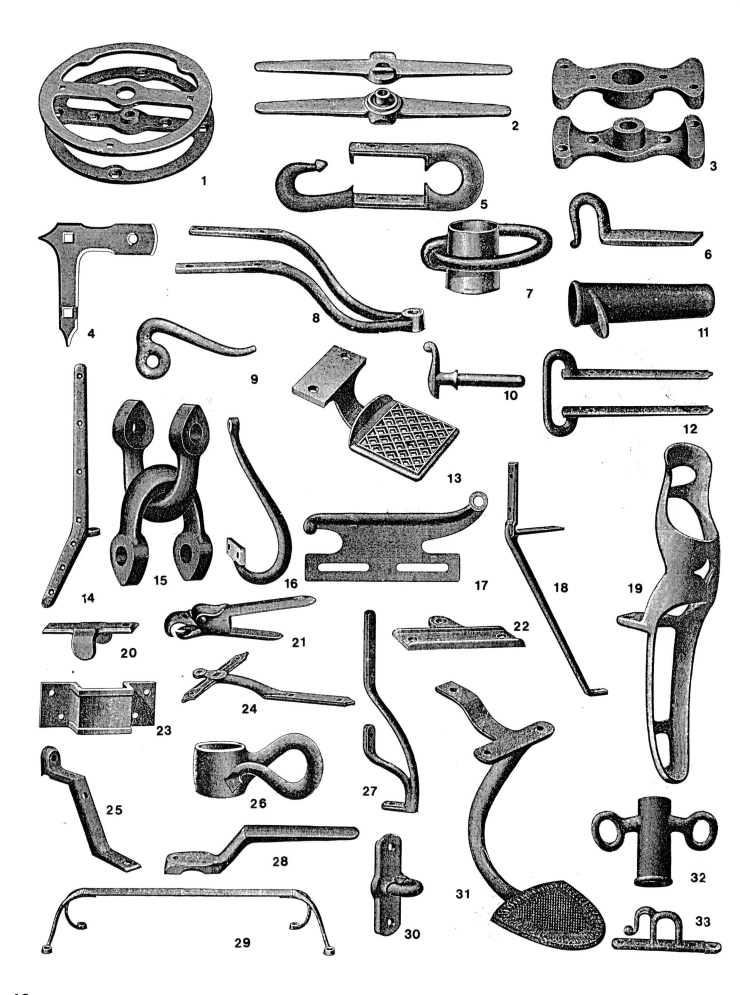

Opposite: Carriage and wagon manufacturers could purchase malleable iron castings for any conceivable use on a vehicle.

Pictured here are only 33 of literally hundreds of shapes and sizes available in a 976-page catalogue published in 1911 by the Eberhard Manufacturing Co. of Cleveland, Ohio. Eberhard said they produced and carried in stock a line of wagon and plow clevises, brakes, cockeyes, buckles, bridle bits, rings, snaps, and carriage, wagon and saddlery hardware.

The availability of these iron parts simplified the building of wagons and buggies or repairing them by local vehicle producers.

1	Fifth Wheel	18	Side extension body brace
2	Platform bolster plate	19	Whip socket
3	Wiffletree couplings	20	Felloe plate
4	Concord perch plate	21	Sleigh iron
5	Doubletree clip	22	Pole pin holder
6	Binding hook	23	Stake pocket
7	Neck yoke ferrule	24	Front perch iron
8	King bolt brace	25	Dash feet
9	End gate hook	26	Whiffle tree hook
10	Wiffletree cockeye	27	Wagon body brace
11	Pole tip	28	Hound clip tie
12	Pole holdback	29	Toe rail
13	Body step	30	Wagon box chain eye
14	Lazy back iron	31	Phaeton step
15	Spring Shackle	32	Pole crab
16	Express Wagon handle	33	Hold back
17	Wear Iron		

— Author's Collection

High Grade Lamps.

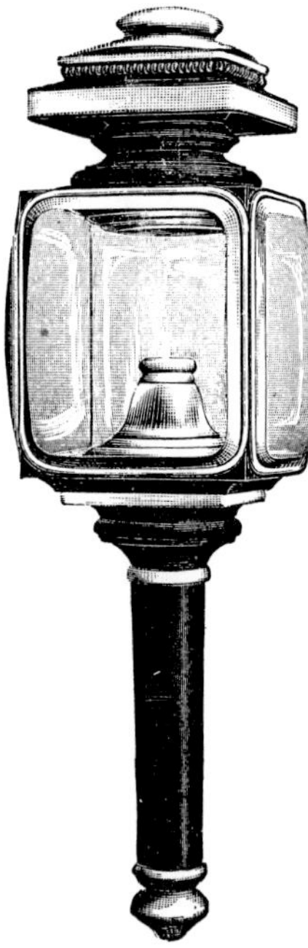

Geneva Square

Oblong body, glasses swelled and round cornered, linings double convex, giving a very rich and white appearance, all the mountings are white metal, and heavily electro plated, thereby preventing any discoloration or show from wear.

LARGE FINGER PROP.

No. 6½,	Glasses,	5 x 6	inches	$16.80	per pair.
No. 7½,	"	5⅜ x 6½	"	18.40	"
No. 8½,	"	5¾ x 7	"	20.60	"
No. 9½,	"	6¼ x 7½	"	22.40	"

A Rich Lamp for Rockaways, Broughams, Landaus, &c.

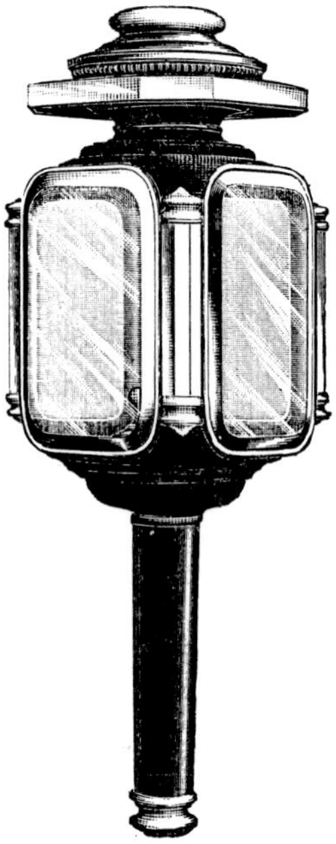

New Castle.

This pattern is one of unique design, having cut glass pillars between the glasses, with silver mountings top and bottom; oblong glasses round cornered. The linings are a double convex variety, and a novelty controlled by our special dies for same. Made in best quality throughout.

LARGE FINGER PROP.

No. 6,	Glasses,	6 x4,	Body	6½ high,	5⅛ wide	21.00	per pair.
No. 7,	"	6½x4½,	"	7 "	5⅝ "	23.50	"
No. 8,	"	7⅛x4⅞,	"	7⅝ "	6 "	25.50	"

Suitable for Rockaways, Broughams, Victorias, &c.

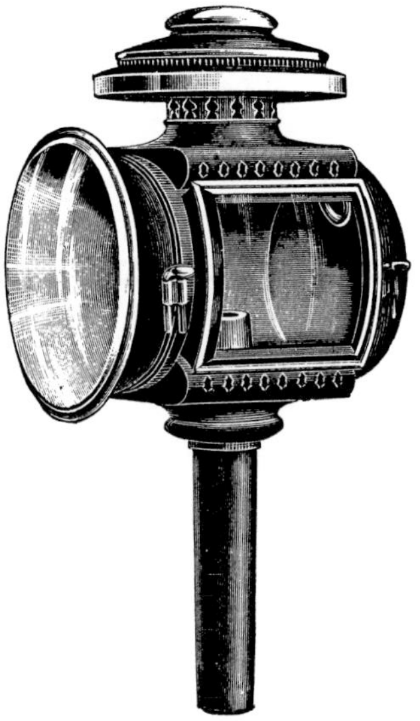

Parisian Mail.

This pattern is considered exceedingly rich, and always in demand, made of the best material, and a fine Lamp in every part, bent side glass, and white metal trimmings throughout.

LARGE FINGER PROP.

No. 5,	diameter of front flange	6½ in.	15.50	per pair.
No. 7	" "	7 "	20.00	"

Used on extension work, Surreys, Coupés, Victorias, and Rockaways.

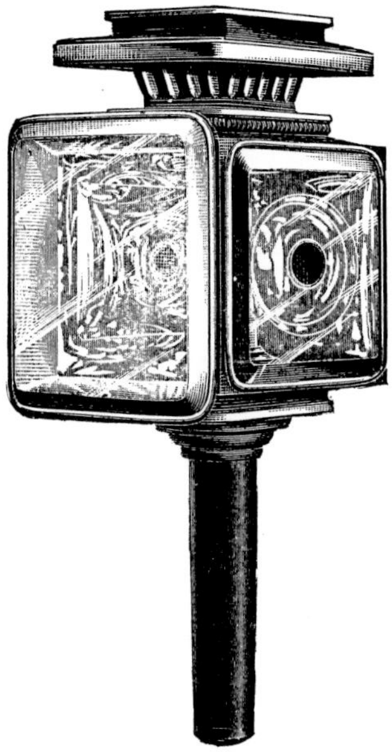

Columbian.

This Lamp is one of the most expensively made Lamps of its size on the market, having in same every feature which tends to make same a work of art as well as usefulness. The linings are the double convex variety, red glass at back, round cornered plate glass in front of flange. In every way of the most perfect workmanship.

PATENT FINGER PROP.

No. 5,	Glass,	3¾x4¾,	Flange. 4½x5	9.65	per pair.
No. 6,	"	4½x5½,	" 5 x5½	11.50	"
No. 7,	"	5 x6	" 5¼x6	16.00	"

Designed for fine Surreys, Extension Carryalls, Rockaways, &c.

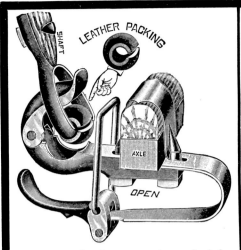

Above: The Bradley Carriage Coupler was advertised in the 1910 American Blacksmith.

— *Author's Collection*

Opposite: Carriage and coach lamps were available in many styles and designs. This group was illustrated in an 1892 catalogue of C.Cowles & Co. in New Haven, Conn.

— *Author's Collection*

Procter & Gamble advertised one of their main products, "Ivory Soap" on the side panel in this 1912 photo. The fine upstanding team of black grade Percherons would be able to haul three or four tons of merchandise on this well painted rig.

The first few pages of this chapter illustrate the horse drawn rigs used by companies whose names are still commonplace today.

— *Philip Weber Collection*

Chapter Two

Handling the Freight

The term "we deliver" had far more meaning in the horse drawn era than it does today.

Daily deliveries to the home were commonplace — oil and kerosene, coal, bakery goods, ice, merchandise ordered from department stores, express and mail to mention a few.

About the only commodities still delivered to the home today are the mail and oil.

For a period of time around 1910, when autos and trucks were coming into prominence, great arguments and debates took place in the press as to which type of service was best. Motorized vehicles had a tendency to break down mechanically. Horse drawn rigs plodded along and delivered the goods.

The various Express Companies favored heavy coach and buggy type horses, the latter weighing 1,100 to 1,250 pounds and the former up to 1,450 pounds. *(Breeder's Gazette, June 30, 1897)*. They did not like the heavy draft types as they were too slow in delivery service. Morgans and Cleveland Bays were considered most durable. Most of the Express Companies prided themselves on fast delivery and needed this type of horse.

Five- to seven-year-old horses were best as they were fully developed and were able to stand the city work.

Teaming companies handled the delivery of merchandise from railroad track and docks to store or factory and from store and factory to freight house with finished goods.

The number of horses used on a vehicle was determined by the size or weight of the load generally carried. One horse on light delivery vehicles was sufficient. Two horses abreast were called a pair and were most common. Four horses, a wheel pair and a lead pair, were referred to as a "team". One horse in the wheel and one in the lead were called a "tandem". Two horses in the wheel and one in the lead were called a "spike" or "unicorn team". No particular name was ever given to a hitch of three horses abreast. Generally, they were called merely a "three horse team" or "three abreast". *(Breeder's Gazette, August 4, 1897)*.

The useful life of a horse in city delivery service was an average of five years. The weakest point of the horse was its feet due to brick pavements. As soon as a horse was unable to do hard work every day, it was sold. Generally they ended up on a farm where, because of working on the soft earth, they had many years of service left.

There is an old adage that "the apparel oft proclaims the man." It was this philosophy that many companies followed in presenting their horses and rigs which they, in turn, felt was excellent advertising.

The New York Biscuit Company used many three abreast hitches of grays and the wagons were all light yellow in color.

James S. Kirk Soap Company and H. J. Heinz Company had white wagons and black Percherons. Armour Packing Company's combination was dappled gray Percherons on yellow wagons. Many local dairy companies preferred white wagons to indicate cleanliness and used black horses whenever available.

Before the days of good highways, the A&P went where the customer lived. Pictured is a turn-of-the-century wagon that delivered tea, coffee, spices and a few other basic commodities to rural patrons who could not get to town to do their grocery shopping.

— *The Great Atlantic & Pacific Tea Co.*

Coal was delivered in canvas buckets as well as in bulk. Conditions on the delivery end would determine which method would be used. Consumers Company was Chicago-based.

— *Philip Weber Collection*

The name "Olson Cartage Co." painted on the front of this wagon means that Borden's leased the rig. The Cartage Company most likely had a large array of vehicles and a huge stable of horses to handle their customers.

— *Philip Weber Collection*

Employee Manual

• Wagonmen will constantly keep as tight a rein as the horses will bear, thus maintaining proper control of them in starting, trotting, walking or stopping.

• Whipping, jerking or abusing horses in any way is forbidden, and if done, will subject the employee at fault to immediate discharge. The Company does not want, nor will it have, any man in charge of horses who is brutal or unkind in his treatment of them.

• Fast driving is strictly forbidden, except when absolutely necessary to connect with trains or boats.

• In driving around corners or over street crossings or railway tracks, horses should not be driven faster than a walk, and must be held under perfect control. Tracks should be crossed at right angles. Before turning corners, wagonmen must signal with the hand or whip when the turn is to be made and in what direction. In turning corners, wagons going to the right should be kept to the right of the center of the street as near the right-hand curb as possible, and vehicles turning to the left should be kept to the right of the center of the two intersecting streets, before turning.

• Wagons must not be stopped suddenly, nor started to turn, without first warning those behind by signal with hand or whip or otherwise.

• Wagonmen must not drive or back their wagons upon the sidewalks of city streets.

• Before turning out or starting from or stopping at the curb line, wagonmen must see that there is sufficient space free from other vehicles so that such turn, start or stop may be safely made, and then give a plainly visible or audible signal.

• In driving in streets where there are car tracks, wagons must not be driven on the track when there is room for them elsewhere.

• To avoid damage or injury to horses, wagons or other property, whether of this Company or others, wagonmen will always take the safe course by avoiding all possible chances of collision, even though they may have to sacrifice their "rights to the road."

• Wagons must be driven on the right side of the street. In meeting vehicles coming from opposite direction, pass to the right. Other vehicles going in the same direction must be passed on the left side.

• Wagonmen must not rein horses either to the right or to the left without first looking behind on the side of the wagon they are to turn, to see that no one is approaching or in the way.

The American Railway Express Co. published an employees manual in the early part of the century. Listed here are a few of the explicit instructions for wagonmen.

— *Wesley Jung
Collection*

Anheuser-Busch had a large assortment of delivery vehicles at their Kansas City branch. This 1894 photo shows wagons for case beer, some for hauling kegs, and a few lightweight rigs for special orders.

— *Anheuser-Busch Co.*

One horse, two horse and four horse wagons are lined up ready for their early morning delivery routes.

The scene is the Anheuser-Busch Kansas City branch in 1894.

— *Anheuser-Busch Co.*

The local bottling companies of Coca Cola products had a variety of horse drawn rigs. Larger vehicles such as pictured here required a team. The product was delivered to the point of sale.

— *Coca Cola Company*

Marshall Field Department Store in Chicago had this beautiful team of roans on the streets in 1913. A team like this could haul many tons of merchandise on this heavy wagon.

— Author's Collection

Johns-Manville Co. of Milwaukee leased this team and wagon and others from Cassel Cartage Co. in 1906. Tony Cassel standing on the wagon said he hauled 500 to 600 tons per day. An outfit like that pictured he said would cost about $1,100 (Wagon - $300; Team - $600; and harness - $200). His most interesting statement was that the wagon would last 25 years with the only service required greasing the wheels.

— Author's Collection

The hoist arrangement could lift the front end of the wagon body, thus simplifying the unloading of coal. If the delivery was to a business establishment and a manhole cover over the coal bin was in the sidewalk, the team could back the wagon to the curb, chutes placed from the rear unloading gate to the coal bin opening, the entire wagon could be unloaded in minutes by lifting the body with the hoist.

— *Author's Collection*

"Lady," says Eric Schneider, driver for the Milwaukee Dairy Distributors, "is the pet of the stable of forty horses." The iron gray mare weighed 1,700 lbs. and was an easygoing good horse for the job of delivering milk and cream. In 1939, when this photo was taken, the Dairy admitted the days of horse drawn rigs was coming to a close. Young fellows coming up won't drive horses. "Below their dignity," they say.

— *Author's photo*

Left: During World War II, the Luick Dairy of Milwaukee put about 40 horse drawn rigs back in service. Tires and gasoline were rationed and trucks scarce. This large team-drawn wagon serviced the restaurants in the downtown area.

— *Author's Photo*

Below: On the go with a load of steel from the Joseph T. Ryerson & Sons Co.

— *Author's Collection*

Left:Rag men toured the residential areas purchasing for a few cents any old clothing or bedding material. They would sort it and stuff it into bags then deliver and sell it to a tradesman who further sorted, washed and sold the rags. Here a days pick up is backed up to a dock for unloading.

— *Author's Photo*

Below: Time out for lunch for both man and horse. Junk peddlers made a living picking up odds and ends discarded as useless then delivering to and selling their loads to collection points.

— *Author's Collection*

Left: The weather is cold and crisp so the driver of this rig broke out the canvas blankets for his team. The horses are heading for the barn at a good trot after completing their route. This is one of many horse drawn milk wagons owned and operated by Milwaukee's Gridley Dairy Co. in the early 1940s.

— *Author's Photo*

Below: The Gem City Dairy of Baraboo, Wis., lines up its entire fleet of delivery vehicles. By 1930, about when this photo was taken, motorized vehicles were beginning to push the last bastion of the horse off the streets.

— *Norm Coughlin Collection*

Left: A snappy rig for residential delivery. Bowman of Chicago favored black horses on their white wagons.

— *Bud Yarke Collection*

Below: In 1920, Chicago's Wieland Dairy Co. operated neat looking milk wagons.

— *Norm Coughlin Collection*

A fine looking team for the Parker wagon. The design of the vehicle body allows the front wheels to cut under when making sharp turns.

— *Ontario Archives*

The rural mail carrier was a very important aspect of every day life. He brought the mail, picked up mail, and occasionally (and unofficially) brought important news and delivered messages down the line.

— *U.S. Postal Service*

Collecting mail that had been deposited in official mail boxes was the job of this postal wagon.

— *Philip Weber Collection*

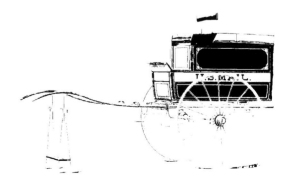

In the early part of the 20th Century, this is the type of turnout used in city service by the Post Office.

— U.S. Postal Service

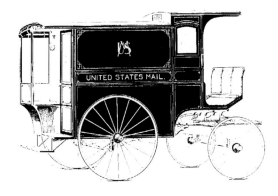

The heavy mail wagon would deliver the sacks of outgoing mail to the depot and the load would be transferred directly into the mail and express railroad car. It took a variety of vehicles to keep the Postal Service operating.

— *U.S. Postal Service*

Before refrigerators, there were ice boxes. To keep these filled and thus preserve food, an elaborate and efficient system was developed.

Ice companies would harvest naturally-made ice from frozen rivers and lakes and ponds. Ice houses were filled with huge blocks of ice — stored in sawdust until needed.

Tons upon tons of block ice were shipped by rail from northern states to those in the south.

In this photo, ice is being harvested in the Milwaukee River above the North Avenue dam. The ice houses in the background extended at least a half mile. The horses are sawing the ice into blocks which will be floated to the conveyors that will carry the blocks into the ice houses.

— *Milwaukee Public Museum*

An ice wagon like this would load up in the morning then cover a specific route to deliver ice. Householders would place a four-sectioned card in their windows that face the street indicating they wanted ice. This card had on it in large letters "25," "50," "75," and "100". If the card was set in the window with the "50" up, then the ice man would deliver a 50 lb. block and place it in the ice box.

— *Norm Coughlin*
Collection

A bigger wagon meant bigger load and, probably a longer route.

— *Norm Coughlin Collection*

Left: Neat looking equipage indicated a sense of pride. Most companies who delivered merchandise to residential neighborhoods kept their wagons in tip top shape.

— *Norm Coughlin Collection*

Below: The tarpaulin covers the blocks of ice and reduces the speed of melting. The three abreast team is exerting its power to move this heavy load up the hill.

— *Norm Coughlin Collection*

Left: Effinger Brewing Co. of Baraboo, Wis., delivered keg beer on a roll wagon. The frame of the wagon body was made up of pipes. A keg could be loaded on the rear end and rolled to the front. Empties were hauled back to the brewery. Note the three kegs hanging under the wagon body.

— Sauk County (Wis.) Historical Society

Below: Vans for moving furniture had big spacious bodies for bulky loads. A full load was not particularly heavy, thus the rather lightweight team.

— Philip Weber Collection

Transporting grapes from the vineyards to processing plant of Welch Foods Inc. These wagons delivered boxes of hand-picked grapes to the plant at Westfield, N.Y. in 1904.

— *Welch Foods, Inc.*

Everyone seems to be posing, at attention for this photo. Note the step down tail gate on the wagons for easier loading of furniture.

— *Philip Weber Collection*

Each farmer had his name or initials painted on the neck of his milk cans. At the creamery, he was credited with his production — later the cans were returned to the various owners for the next days' supply.

— *National Archives*

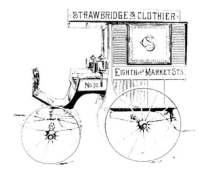

Left: The owners, bakers and neatly-dressed salesmen pose for their photo. The one horse delivery wagons are neat and trim. Circa 1900.

— *Metropolitan Toronto Library Board*

Below: Load after load of baskets of tomatoes wait to be unloaded at processing plant of Campbell Soup Co.

— *Campbell Soup Co.*

Even the seat next to the driver has a crate of merchandise as this team sets off on its delivery schedule with its bulky load.

— *Norm Coughlin Collection*

Left: Just about every business establishment, no matter how small, had a horse and wagon with which to deliver orders.

Peck & Herfort Dry Goods & Groceries was located in Baraboo, a town of about 6,000 in southcentral Wisconsin.

— *Sauk County (Wis.) Historical Society*

Below: Ready to roll out on their daily city deliveries, these wagons would cover the industries, or the general stores or residences. Oil, kerosene or gasoline were delivered in quantities required by the householder.

— *Philip Weber Collection*

Left: Oil, kerosene for lamps, and axle grease were delivered to homes and retail stores by Standard Oil in rigs like this. The tanks were compartmentalized and the drain valves were at the rear of the truck. The rolls of canvas on top of the tank are horse blankets in case of inclement weather.

— *Philip Weber Collection*

Below: For delivery in the business area, larger tank wagons were used, requiring a three abreast team.

— *Standard Oil Co.*

The plumed horse and fascinating sign mounted on the wagon indicate this turnout was to be in a parade.

The Adams Express Co. was a big operator in the hauling and transferring of merchandise.

— *Pennsylvania Historical Society*

From this photo, it looks as though Kent, Ohio, had an early version of the UPS system of today.

Five neat and clean delivery wagons with well matched horses and tidily dressed drivers were most likely a well-known sight around town.

— *Philip Weber Collection*

Left: A well packed load of merchandise on a wagon of Dominion Express Co. of Toronto.

— Canadian Pacific Railroad

Below: The loaded wagon stands in front of the Adams Express Co. stables. This conveyance is ready for a local parade — note the plumes on the horses — thus the trunks on the load are labeled with the various divisions, all of which emphasize the size of the company.

— Pennsylvania Historical Society

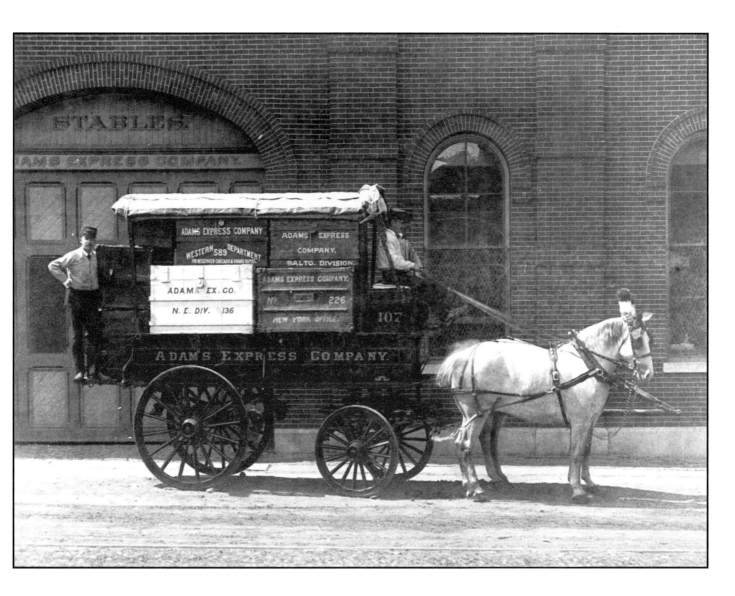

Horses clopped over brick pavements in Chicago in 1891.

— *Author's Collection*

Chapter Three

Traffic Problems and Road Building

During the horse drawn era there were traffic jams, speeders, slow-pokes and smart aleck drivers. One sage commented "there were just as many dumb drivers but fewer accidents because the horses were smarter."

There were speed limits, and they varied from city to city.

San Fransisco regulations said horses could move not faster than a walk over street crossings. Immoderate driving was forbidden. In parks the speed limit was 10 mph.

In Chicago, the speed limit was 6 mph, but when turning corners it was reduced to 4 mph. In the winter Snow Racing was permitted on certain Boulevards.

Boston law said not more than 7 mph, except in outlying districts, where 12 mph was permitted.

Detroit allowed 6 mph except on special streets designated for speeding.

Out in the country roads were in such shape that their condition usually controlled the speeds.

There might be signs that would proclaim "Keep out of the ruts and save the road." Everyone was urged to wear down the high places and make the road smooth. It was a test of high citizenship when a man sought to keep his wheels out of the damaging ruts.

There seemed to be a push for wide tires on wagons. The feeling was that the wide tires would pack the road while the narrow wheels tended to cut into the surface.

In some areas, where a supply of trees was plentiful, plank roads were constructed. Their advantage was that they provided all weather travel. The spring thaw or low bog areas did not slow up traffic on these plank roads, which usually charged a toll.

Realizing the trials and tribulations of these early days, one wonders how commerce moved or how anything got done.

However, while there have been improvements in the quality of roads and in highway speeds, one has to wonder if city traffic problems are much improved today.

Horses did, indeed, cause street pollution — tons of it. However, the manure could be swept up and recycled to good advantage.

Today, we have pollution — tons of it. And the smog hangs in the air and can't be swept away — and surely can't be recycled.

From the way traffic seems to be stalled and people are standing in the street and on wagons, some kind of a parade is approaching in this street scene in Philadelphia in 1897. The cart in the foreground is most likely a city vehicle. The driver's job is probably the all-important task of picking up manure.

— National Archives

A busy street near the freight depot. Many types of vehicles are delivering or on the way to pick up loads. New York, 1901.

— *Author's Collection*

Accidents did occur. A yapping dog probably spooked the horse and during the resulting runaway, the wagon lurched and crashed into a light pole spewing its load of bottled milk along the sidewalk. This unfortunate accident occurred in Elgin, Ill. in 1925.

— *Norm Coughlin Collection*

The horse, which had broken away from the wagon, continued its galloping spree for about six blocks before cooling off and, wondering where his driver and wagon was, returned to the scene of the crash.

— *Norm Coughlin Collection*

Studebaker Bros. Mfg. Co. offered a large assortment of vehicles for road work. Available were water sprinklers, street sweepers and road oilers. An example of the latter seen here was illustrated in their 1909 catalogue. Controlling the oil streams was the job of the man who occupied the rear seat.

— Wesley Jung Collection

The Studebaker street sweeper had an adjustable brush so the dirt and manure could be swept toward the curb. Men with two-wheeled carts then removed the refuse from the street.

— Wesley Jung Collection

The speed of a walking horse is generally considered to be 3-1/2 miles per hour. Photos of street scenes such as this one in Milwaukee in the late 1880's gives the feeling there was no sense of urgency. It was a slow but sure approach.

— *Milwaukee Public Museum*

Left: Most cities provided water wagons to keep down the dust and to wash the manure accumulation into the gutters.

— *Milwaukee Public Museum*

Below:A catalogue page from the Kindling Machinery Co. of Milwaukee, circa 1910, showed their street cleaner. The city of Milwaukee had 10 units in service and officials from the city of Houston, Texas, said "It wastes no water, creates no dust, sweeps clean and revolving rubber squeegee washes pavement so thoroughly that it leaves no slime, mud or dust in its wake.

— *Author's Collection*

There were many styles and types of street cleaning equipment available. This sweeper was manufactured by the Universal Road Machinery Co. of Kingston, New York in 1913. The vehicle had, as optional equipment, a large water tank and sprinkling device to keep down the dust as the sweeper revolved.

— *Author's Collection*

A busy street scene, circa 1890. In the photo are delivery vehicles, heavy dray wagons, cabs, a coach and an express wagon. With no "Stop & Go Lights," traffic on the cross street was a problem. Perhaps the mounted policeman's duties included controlling the flow of vehicles.

— *Henry Ford Museum*

Busy New York street scene. Patient horses stand with their rigs backed up to docks. Out in the middle of the street is a bustle of wagons heading to pick up a load or delivering one.

— Motor Vehicle Manufacturers Association

A cluster of drays waiting their turn to unload. The variety of draft animals range from a team of small mules to a handsome single, to a well fed team of dapple grays, to a scrawny black. Note immediately behind the load of baled excelsior is a chain-driven truck.

— *Motor Vehicle Manufacturers Association*

Laying asphalt on Broadway Street in Milwaukee in 1895. A team has brought a load of hot asphalt which will be raked level, ready for the steam roller to compact it.

— *Milwaukee Public Museum*

Left: These three ladies had their trip to town cut short. It appears that the wheel collapsed.

— *Milwaukee Public Library*

The Old South Water Street Market at Chicago in 1922
really indicates about the last major use of horses except for
some horse drawn milk wagons used by the large Dairies.
Visible in the photograph are about 40 horse drawn rigs and
30 trucks.

— *National Archives*

A fascinating street scene of the 1880's in New York. The view of Broadway at Maiden Lane shows Omnibuses, heavy dray wagons, light delivery wagons, a hand cart, and men carrying sandwich boards.

— *Library of Congress*

The farmer's market at Troy, New York in 1910. The horses were lined up facing each other so the rear or business end of the wagons became an aisle. Farmers would come in from the outlying areas about 5 a.m. daily. By 9 a.m., business would be brisk and by 11 a.m., everyone would be gone.

— *Gene Baxter Collection*

Milwaukee's Union Depot in 1890. Carriages and cabs lined up at the curb while horse drawn street cars plied the rails to other sections of the city.

— *Milwaukee Public Museum*

A bustling view of New York's dock area. Merchandise is piled on the edge of the dock waiting for a dray wagon.

— *Dover Publications*

Generally speaking, paved roads were non-existent out in the country. The spring thaw or even a heavy rain would create miserable going for traffic.

— *Watertown (Wis.) Historical Society*

In building streets and roads in the era of 1910, two-wheeled scrapers cuffed off the topsoil or delivered crushed stone.

— *National Archives*

To unload a dirt wagon, the side boards were lifted from the bolsters. Then the floor of the wagon, which was made from a series of 4 x 4's, were jostled up through the material which would allow it to fall to the ground. The ends of the 4 x 4's would be tapered to enable the men to get a good grip on them. When the load was dumped, the body would be put back together and the teamster headed out for another load.

— *Author's Collection*

Right: The rig in the center, down in the mud by 6", is hauling a load to the railroad depot. The driver on the left is lashing his horse to get it through the muddy road.

— *State Historical Society of Wisconsin*

Dump wagons were efficient and practical. By tripping a lever, the hinged bottom would flop open and release the load. As the wagon moved on, the driver would crank the bottom halves back into position and lock them so they're ready for the next load.

— *Author's Collection*

In 1914, the rock formation made for hard and miserable work in Wilmington, Del. Breaking up the stone to manageable sizes was tough going.

— *Motor Vehicle Manufacturers Association*

Street building in Milwaukee. This 1912 scene shows a steam shovel scooping up dirt, swinging around, and dumping the earth into a waiting wagon. Progress was slow but steady.

— *Milwaukee Journal*

Away from the hustle and bustle of the big cities, life was more peaceful. A good steady farm team was a necessity for hauling or hitching to the family carriage for a Sunday church picnic.

— *Warren Broderick Collection*

An ignominious end to a jaunt in the country. And this item appeared in the Aug. 2, 1899 issue of the *Breeder's Gazette.* "The joke of the season is on Mr. and Mrs. William K. Vanderbilt, Jr., who started for Narragansett Pier in an automobile and came back in a farmer's wagon. As they neared the ferry at Jamestown, a field of mud was before them and into it Mr. Vanderbilt dashed, hoping to get through it in a rush. The vehicle, however, was so inconsiderate as to stop right in the middle of it. Some farmers dug the automobile out and brought the Vanderbilts to Newport in a wagon."

— *Anna Fox Collection*

Because of very specialized requirements, many of the large railroad circuses constructed wagons in their own shops. Wagon No. 44 carrying a load of quarter poles is an example of the massive, heavily-ironed construction used by Ringling Bros. and Barnum & Bailey Circus. Note the spare wheel hanging under the wagon. On top of the load are a couple of stake pullers.

— *Circus World Museum*

Chapter Four

Hauling Unusual Loads

In this chapter, we will consider the unusual loads that horses were asked to move. But instead of milk, ice or bread, it is a house, a 21-ton cylinder block or huge blocks of granite from a quarry.

With the correct use of horsepower, combined with winches, capstans and cables, anything could be moved or hauled and was, as the photographs will show.

Massive and heavy loads hauled over bricks, paved streets, or hard-packed roads, eased the burden for the horses and problems for the men.

When moving mining equipment, boilers, pumps, timbers, hoists and stamping mills up into the mountains over rough terrain, through valleys, gulleys and gulches, where there was a semblance of a trail, the job became formidable.

The horses and mules, when properly used, were able to accomplish their tasks — roads or no roads.

The big railroad circuses faced rough conditions on a daily basis. Their massively built and heavily loaded wagons were moved from the streets to the showgrounds. If the lot was soft from rain, or sandy, the six or possibly eight-horse team would have difficulty spotting the wagon in its place. The boss hostler would call in another eight-horse team and hook on to a heavy steel ring on the corner of the vehicle. If more horsepower was needed, another eight would be whistled in. These were called hook rope teams.

The circus drivers were all expert horsemen. They never discouraged a team by letting them struggle with a load that was obviously beyond their capacity to move. Extra sixes and eights were added when the ground was soft and then the Percherons got the job done. These teams were faced with varying conditions on a daily basis as the circus travelled from town to town.

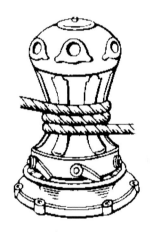

Capstan

If it is a house you wanted moved, a team could do it with the assistance of a couple of capstans. Horse power rotated the vertical spindle mounted drums winding the rope around them and leveraging the house down the hill. This scene took place in 1908 in San Fransisco.

— *Milwaukee Public Museum*

It took 40 horses and 20 teamsters to move this massive 21-ton load. It was a cast iron bed plate or cylinder block for a compressor to move natural gas in a pipeline for the Ohio Fuel Gas Co. at Utica, Ohio. Photo was taken in 1903.

— *Merle H. Grant Collection*

Hook roping a heavily-loaded Cole Bros. Circus wagon over soft ground. The drivers always sat on the near wheel horse of their eight or six-horse teams. The photo was taken in 1940.

— *Jerry Booker Photo*

The logging industry used horses long before tractors were introduced into the woods This 1897 photo shows how logs were snaked out of the forest.

— *Mendocino County* (Calif.) *Historical Society*

The team was struggling to snake this heavy log into the road area in Tehama County, California.

— *Siskiyou County (Calif.) Historical Society*

Log Carts were designed to move heavy logs out of the forest area. The large wheels straddled the log and rolled easily over the rough terrain. One manufacturer of log carts, Gabriel Streich, Co. of Oshkosh, Wis., produced such units with wheel diameters ranging from nine to twelve feet. All wheels had steel tires six inches wide.

— *National Agriculture Library*
Forest Service Photo Colection

Left: Sixteen horses hauled an enormous load of logs out of the woods in 1895 in Siskiyou County, Calif.

— *Meriam Library California State University, Chico*

Below: Horses hauled piling out of the forest to the Noyo River in Mendocino County, Calif. Many of these pilings were 100 to 125 feet long.

— *Mendocino County (Calif.) Historical Society*

Freighting in Montana in 1883. There appears to be four wagons hooked together that the 12 horses are pulling.

— *Philip Weber Collection*

A heavy granite monument being moved over Troy, New York, city streets to the Oakwood Cemetery in 1879. Four drivers are seen handling the horses.

— *Gene Baxter Collection*

Left: A stack of 202 bales of Wyoming hay weighed 19,640 pounds and created a very topheavy load. Photo was taken in 1909.

— *Author's Collection*

Below: Moving day for some householder — perhaps the man walking along side the wagon.

— *Milwaukee Public Museum*

A freight caravan moving across the prairie near Malta, Mont., in 1905.

The load includes a Singer Sewing Machine for some lucky housewife.

— *Milwaukee Public Museum*

A wool outfit on the plains near Great Falls, Mont., in 1902.

— Milwaukee Public Museum

Bell Telephone used this specially-built wagon with its low-slung body for hauling heavy reels of cable.

— *Philip Weber Collection*

Three horses move eight rail trams loaded with boards at this saw mill in Mendocino, Calif. (c. 1912).

— *Mendocino County (Calif.) Historical Society*

Mining equipment being hauled in the area of Cascade, Idaho, around 1910. The size of the wheels indicate the mammoth loads these vehicles could carry over very rough terrain. Seven teams were required for this freight.

— *Idaho Historical Society*

A placer mine ordered a boiler which was shipped by rail to Weiser, Idaho. From there, it required horses to move the bulky equipment to where it was needed.

— *Idaho Historical Society*

A wagon load of ties being hauled from the forest, where they were cut, to the railroad siding.

— *Mendocino County (Calif.) Historical Society*

Left: On a big load, Gridley Dairy Co. of Milwaukee, used a five-horse team. The wagon is carrying approximately 180 cans of milk weighing about six tons or more.

— *Richard Mueller Collection.*

Below: The dead weight blocks of granite required a specially-designed wagon used in the quarry.

— *Henry Ford Museum*

Off-loading a valuable shipment at the U.S. Treasury Building in Washington, D.C. The size of the wheels as well as the three-abreast team indicates that this vehicle was designed to carry very heavy loads.

— *Henry Ford Museum*

Artist E.L. Henry depicted travelling through New York's Shawangunk Mountains in the Hudson River Valley (1881). Travel by horse drawn coach was not confined to the western states.

— *Haggin Museum, Stockton, California*

Chapter Five

Moving People

Whether ridden or driven, it was the horse that kept the economy going by hauling people to their jobs. Horses moved material into factories and finished products out.

As America developed and expanded westward, horses were on hand to get people where they wanted to go. Considering road construction of the times the horse drawn equipment was extremely efficient.

The hazards of unpaved roads, lack of bridges, holdups by highwaymen and Indian attacks did not stop the flow of people in their westward migration.

Livery stables could be found in every town, large or small, where horses and buggies could be rented. These same liverys would board horses for people who had no facilities to stable horses at their homes. Stage lines were established. Many were for short runs between two major cities with stops at each town or village between.

In the west, a network of Stage Lines covered hundreds of miles so efficiently that teams could be changed about every 15 miles. This enabled the drivers to keep their teams of four or six at a trot or gallop the entire stint. Within the cities, cabs, omnibuses, and later horse cars on rails, provided mass transportation for the public.

Today, when we travel there seems to be plenty of aggravations, annoyances and vexations with jammed parking lots, crowded airports, endless delays, lost baggage and dirty lunch counters.

A century ago, when travelling cross country in a Concord Coach behind six galloping horses, it wasn't all peaches and cream either.

Read this fascinating gem that was printed in the Oct. 3, 1877, Omaha Herald and provided here by Bob Chandler, head of the Wells Fargo Bank History Room:

"Never ride in cold weather with tight boots or shoes, nor close-fitting gloves. Bathe your feet before starting in cold water, and wear loose overshoes and gloves two or three sizes too large. When the driver asks you to get off and walk, do it without grumbling. He will not request it unless absolutely necessary.

If a team runs away, sit still and take your chances; if you jump, nine times out of ten you will be hurt. In very cold weather, abstain entirely from liquor while on the road; a man will freeze twice as quick while under its influence. Don't growl at food stations; stage companies generally provide the best they can get. Don't keep the stage waiting; many a virtuous man has lost his character by so doing. Don't smoke a strong pipe inside, especially in the morning; spit on the leeward side of the coach.

If you have anything to take in a bottle, pass it around; a man who drinks by himself in such a case is lost to all human feeling. Provide stimulants before starting; ranch whisky is not always nectar. Be sure and take two heavy blankets with you; you will need them. Don't swear, nor lop over on your neighbor when sleeping. Don't ask how far it is to the next station until you get there. Take small change to pay expenses. Never attempt to fire a gun or pistol while on the road; it may frighten the team and careless handling and cocking of the weapon makes nervous people nervous.

Don't discuss politics or religion, nor point out places where horrible murders have been committed, if delicate women are among the passengers. Don't linger too long at the pewter wash basin at the station. Don't grease your hair before starting or dust will stick there in sufficient quantities to make a respectable "tater" patch. Tie a silk handkerchief around your neck to keep out dust and prevent sunburns.

Don't imagine for a moment you are going on a picnic; expect annoyance, discomfort, and some hardships. If you are disappointed, thank heaven."

Cabs line up at the Elmira, New York, railroad station in the 1890's. They were called "hacks" and the driver would charge 50¢ a head to take passengers where they wanted to go.

— *Author's Collection*

No. 575—PLATFORM WAGONETTE, WITH GLASS SIDES AND ENDS.

The above cut shows our full platform wagonette. This style is used by liverymen and hotels for the transfer of passengers, in preference to omnibuses or any other kind of wagon. It is light, easy riding, noiseless, easy to get into, and can be turned around in short space. Seats eight passengers comfortably inside, two outside. Has 1⅜-inch double collar steel axles; 1⅜-inch Sarven patent wheels. Glass of sides are set in frames; the frames can be taken out in hot weather and the curtains used; the center glass in front drops down s › passengers can speak to driver. The glass in rear door also drops down, giving good ventilation when side windows are in. Large space in front of driver's seat for carrying trunks, valises, etc., made very strong and substantial. Roof is lined with dark green, all-wool cloth, with fringe to match. Seats are trimmed with leather. Has good carpet in bottom of body and under seats; large oil burning lamps; stiff pole.

Same every way as others sell for $300.00 to $350.00 on four months'

time. We make our price low, so anyone who may not have the money can afford to borrow it at the bank and buy of us. Remember we will save you at least $100.00.

We letter your name, or the name of your livery, or hotel, on the inside and outside of the door, free.

Three per cent discount on No. 575 for cash in advance amounts to $6.00, and almost all of our customers send money with the order to save this amount. When the full amount is not sent with order we ask for at least enough to cover freight both ways.

Price, C. O. D., with stiff pole, oil burning
  lamps, glass sides, including curtains.......**$200.00**
Price, cash with order........................... 194.00
Extra for brake.................................   8.00

In their 1899 catalogue, the Elkhart Carriage & Harness Mfg. Co. illustrated this platform wagonette for $200. A rig of this type was used by liverymen and hotels for transferring passengers. It seated eight passengers.

— Author's Collection

An 1883 Harper's Weekly depicted this late afternoon drive in New York Central Park with a great array of elegant turnouts. This ritual was, in effect, a promenade for pleasure and a chance to show off magnificent horses and handsome equipage.

— *Author's Collection*

The drawing is titled "Ninety in the Shade" and appeared in the July 19, 1890 issue of Harper's Weekly. The accompanying story mentioned that there have been erected in New York streets by public and private agencies some 150 troughs where horses could be watered. The Society for the Prevention of Cruelty to Animals has a force of 10 men engaged at points where their services are most called upon for the prevention of abuse. The report from Chicago was that horses were dying so fast in the streets from overwork in the heat that the authorities did not command the means to remove the bodies. Most New York streetcar companies had established relief stations for their horses. This illustration represents one of the shaded areas provided.

— *Author's Collection*

Typical open-sided horse car. Note step running length of the car. It was built by John Stephenson & Co. in New York.

— *Smithsonian Collection*

The Mt. Shasta Stage Line (c. 1901) in Northern California. The dust churning up from the horses' hooves and revolving wheels created one of the many discomforts of this form of travel. Rain would settle the dust. Too much rain turned the roads into quagmires.

— *Wells Fargo Bank History Room*

The Baltimore & Ohio Railroad provided vehicles like this to transfer passengers from one station in Baltimore to the other. Frequently, hotels owned or rented such vehicles to bring guests from depots to the inn.

— *Smithsonian Institution*

Boonville, New York depot with omnibuses from the hotels lined up waiting for expected trains and their passengers.

— *Ron Ryder Collection*

About 1885 in Milwaukee. The team on the horse car is moving at a good trot. This could be done where traffic was light and the tracks were clear.

— *H. H. Bennett Studio*

Citizens Passenger Railway operated in Pittsburgh. The driver has his right hand on the brake lever and the reins in his left hand.

— *Carnegie Library of Pittsburgh*

Frequently, liveries would own horsedrawn funeral equipment, as well as a complete line of vehicles for other uses.

— *State Historical Society of Wisconsin*

A full load. Ten people plus baggage are visible on top of the large coach. Probably another 9 or 10 persons are inside. A load like this required the 8-horse-hitch. The coach was leaving Calistoga in Napa County, Calif., in 1909, and heading north to Lake County.

— *Robert Chandler Collection*

A stage carrying U.S. Mail and Wells Fargo express is about to leave the National Hotel in Jackson, Calif. (c. 1893). It is the Sutter Creek and Jackson Stageline. The Wells Fargo messenger with a shotgun in his lap rides on the driver's left.

— *Wells Fargo Bank History Room*

An 1867 Wells Fargo timetable and price schedule.

— *Wells Fargo Bank History Room*

This stage could carry nine people inside and it operated between Sparta and Black River Falls, Wis., in 1863. The photo was taken on Sparta's main street.

— *Milwaukee Journal*

Harlowton, Mont., stage in 1903 using an Abbot-Downing mud wagon. The horses are moving into a gallop on a cold day, indicated by the well-bundled driver.

— *Montana Historical Society*

OVERLAND MAIL ROUTE
TO CALIFORNIA.

Through in Six Days to Sacramento!

CONNECTING WITH THE DAILY STAGES

To all the Interior Mining Towns in Northern California and Southern Oregon.
Ticketed through from PORTLAND, by the

OREGON LINE OF STAGE COACHES!

And the Rail Road from Oroville to Sacramento,

Passing through Oregon City, Salem, Albany, Corvallis, Eugene City, Oakland,
Winchester, Roseburg, Canyonville, Jacksonville, and in California—
Yreka, Trinity Centre, Shasta, Red Bluff, Tehama, Chico,
Oroville, Marysville to SACRAMENTO.

TRAVELERS AVOID RISK of OCEAN TRAVEL

Pass through the HEART OF OREGON—the Valleys of Rogue River, Umpqua and Willamette.

This portion of the Pacific Slope embraces the most BEAUTIFUL and attractive, as well as some of the most BOLD, GRAND and PICTUERESQUE SCENERY on the Continent. The highest snow-capped mountains, (Mt. HOOD, Mt. SHASTA and others,) deepest ravines and most beautiful valleys.

Stages stop over one night at JACKSONVILLE and YREKA, for passengers to rest. Passengers will be permitted to lay over at any point, and resume their seats at pleasure, any time within one month.

FARE THROUGH, FIFTY DOLLARS.

Ticket Office at Arrigoni's Hotel, Portland.

H. W. CORBETT & Co.,

Proprietors Oregon Stage Line.

PORTLAND, July 19, 1866.

W. D. Carter, Printer, Front St., Portland, Oregon.

In 1866, the Oregon Stage Line distributed advertisements
like this in the towns and villages they serviced.

— *Wesley Jung Collection*

105

Above: The Central Pacific Railroad's busy depot at Cisco, Calif., in 1867.

The Wells Fargo Pioneer Stage Co. has three well-loaded Concord Coaches ready to roll out. The roof racks are stacked with baggage as are, no doubt, the rear boots.

In this period of time, some stage lines allowed each passenger 25 pounds of baggage, while others allowed 30 pounds. Any weight in excess of these stated amounts were charged perhaps $1 per pound extra.

— *Wells Fargo Bank History Room*

Opposite: An advertisement for stage service in 1810 from Boston to points south.

— *Author's Collection*

BOSTON,
Plymouth & Sandwich
MAIL STAGE,

CONTINUES TO RUN AS FOLLOWS:

LEAVES Boston every Tuesday, Thursday, and Saturday mornings at 5 o'clock, breakfast at Leonard's, Scituate ; dine at Bradford's, Plymouth; and arrive in Sandwich the same evening. Leaves Sandwich every Monday, Wednesday and Friday mornings ; breakfast at Bradford's, Plymouth; dine at Leonard's, Scituate, and arrive in Boston the same evening.

Passing through Dorchester, Quincy, Wyemouth, Hingham, Scituate, Hanover, Pembroke, Duxbury, Kingston, Plymouth to Sandwich. *Fare,* from Boston to Scituate, 1 doll. 25 cts. From Boston to Plymouth, 2 dolls. 50 cts. From Boston to Sandwich, 3 dolls. 63 cts.

N. B. Extra Carriages can be obtained of the proprietor's, at Boston and Plymouth, at short notice.— ☞STAGE BOOKS kept at Boyden's Market-square, Boston, and at Fessendon's, Plymouth.

LEONARD & WOODWARD.

BOSTON, *November* 24, 1810.

Waiting for the train is depicted in this lovely painting by artist E.L. Henry. The South Orange, New Jersey, depot of the Morris and Essex Railroad is a busy place. A boy hurries his sheep across the tracks as he sees the oncoming train. On the left, a carriage and wagon await arriving friends. The depot platform is filled with people, some ready to leave town, others waiting to greet arriving friends. On the right is a waiting stage coach that will take passengers to outlying villages.

— *Chase Manhattan Bank*

In the 1880's, the Abbot-Downing Co. built this beautiful coach for the Glen's Falls and Lake George Stage Co. in New York.

Including the driver, this vehicle could probably carry 24 or more people.

— *New Hampshire Historical Society*

The Downieville Stage Co. operated this Mudwagon in Sierra County, Calif. In the background is the Mountain House Inn for weary travellers. The couple is about to depart. The woman has her hand on the stage's portable step.

— *Wells Fargo Bank History Room*

The "Rubberneck" wagons in 1901 in Milwaukee were provided for the passengers of the S. S. Virginia. The sight-seeing vehicles could accommodate 30 to 40 people. The fare was 75¢.

These enormous rigs were called Columbian Coaches because they were built for the World's Columbian Exposition of 1893 in Chicago. There were ten of them that ran from the uptown hotels to Jackson Park. Each weighed 6,000 pounds and were built in Quincy, Illinois, at a cost of $3,000 each.

After the Fair, Hebard Warehouse and Van Co. purchased five for coaching parties and picnics in the parks. In Chicago, they were referred to as "leviathans of the boulevards."

— *Milwaukee Public Museum*

Above: The slack in the traces indicates that the team is pulling up (stopping). The wheel skid or drag shoe was positioned under the left rear wheel at the top of a severe hill. Skidding the wheel was sufficient braking for coaches of this type. When the chains and skid were released, they were again hung on a hook under the body.

— *Author's Collection*

Below: The reinsman or whip seems unperturbed as he handles his four-in-hand through the street. The artist, R. Caton Woodville, captured the action of the spirited team in his drawing dated 1892.

Elkhart Carriage Co. said about this vehicle "One must see it to appreciate its beauty." The body was painted black and a rich shade of green. The running gear was dark Brewster green with neat trimming.

— *Author's Collection*

In 1899, the Elkhart Carriage & Harness Mfg. Co. listed this Stanhope.

— *Author's Collection*

G & D Cook & Co. of New Haven, Conn., illustrated this family coach in their 1860 catalogue. It was priced at $600 to $800, depending on the options the buyer chose.

— *Author's Collection*

In 1909, Montgomery Ward advertised this buggy.

— *Author's Collection*

Almost hidden among the ads for buggies, farm wagons and running gear is an advertisement for an auto. One of their claims is "No crawling under the car to make adjustments." These advertisements were in a 1909 Breeder's Gazette.

— *Author's Collection*

SOLID COMFORT SURREYS

1908 STYLES HIGH GRADE SURREYS

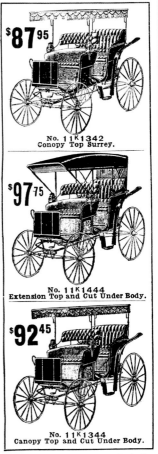

$87⁹⁵

No. 11K1342
Conopy Top Surrey.

$97⁷⁵

No. 11K1444
Extension Top and Cut Under Body.

$92⁴⁵

No. 11K1344
Canopy Top and Cut Under Body.

$93⁹⁵

No. 11K1442

Covered by our three-year guarantee against defect in material or workmanship.

DESCRIPTION OF No. 11K1442

SEATS. Latest style auto seats, very roomy and comfortable; high polished solid panel over-stuffed spring backs; seat cushions are of the box frame pattern, fitted with plenty of Staple & Hanford soft coil springs, making the job very easy riding; upholstered seat ends; seats are braced and reinforced throughout; upholstered in either a heavy 16-ounce all wool imported dark green body cloth or extra grade upholstering leather, according to the section of the country to which it is shipped. If you have any preference be sure to specify in your order, otherwise we will upholster in the material best suited for the section of the country to which it is shipped.

BODY. Large, roomy and comfortable body, made of the best material obtainable for the purpose; 6 feet 1 inch long by 28 inches wide; hardwood frame; seasoned ash sills; hardwood corner posts, uprights and seat frame; sills reinforced the entire length with a heavy steel rocker plate; hardwood skirting back and front seats; the step boards are put in in the most substantial manner, carefully fitted; body has a very nice belt or moulding, as shown in the illustration; body and seat panels are seasoned poplar with rounded corners; seat rods are bolted through sills; full length velvet carpet in bottom of body; large steps; patent leather double fenders; handsome oil burning lamps; padded leather dash.

TOP. Large, handsome, removable leather quarter extension top of the most improved pattern; quarters are very wide, running the full length from front to back, made of the best grade of black enameled top leather; back stays carefully padded and lined with a good heavy wool lining; the roof and back curtain of this top are made of an extra heavy quality

of rubber; a very handsome raised valance is used, front and rear; long curved top joints; large black prop nuts; top throughout is lined with an all wool very heavy dark green head lining; the back curtain is lined with the same material; the top has full length side and back curtains; auto curtain fasteners; enameled bow sockets; in fact, the top throughout is made of the best class material, to correspond with the balance of the job; waterproof storm apron. Top is fitted so it can be removed instantly without the use of tools.

GEAR. 1⅛-inch axles, made of refined steel, the axles are of the drop pattern, tested in our micrometer gauge, so that they all have the same pitch, so that they will all set perfectly, so that our job will run easy and track true. The spindles are of the long distance dust and mudproof collar pattern; the axles are fitted with a heavy hickory axle cap, which is cemented, sanded and clipped to the axle with wrought iron clips; large full bearing fifth wheel is used, to which is connected two wood reaches, which run to the rear axle, where they are connected with wrought iron stay braces; these reaches are ironed full length; the springs are four-plate front and five-plate rear, made of the best oil tempered spring steel, 36 inches in length, fully guaranteed, of the open head elliptic pattern; to the front spring is clipped a wood spring bar, which is attached to the body; to the rear spring is clipped wood spring bar; there is a steel strip running the full length of the body, connecting the front spring bar and the rear body loop.

WHEELS. We use a good substantial 1-inch surrey wheel on this job, of the Sarven's patent style; spokes are made of selected second growth hickory, fully guaranteed. To keep the rims from split-

ting we put a screw on each side of the spokes in the rim. When furnished with steel tires the wheels are fitted with an oval edge steel tire, and a bolt runs clear through the rim and tire between each spoke; the tires are heated before being put on the wheel, making the strongest kind of a wheel made. We furnish regular, wheels 38 inches front and 42 inches rear. Can furnish wheels 40 inches front and 44 inches rear if ordered. Can also furnish the Columbus staggered spoke wheel for $1.50 extra. (See page 92).

SHAFTS. Extra grade XXX second growth hickory shafts, trimmed with genuine leather 30 inches back from the point, four leather squares and oval straps; double braced; Bradley shaft couplers.

PAINTING. Every attention is paid to each little detail to make this one of the handsomest, most attractive and stylish jobs of painting that ever went out of any factory; we use more care to get a smooth finish on the body and gear; use more coats of painting, rubbing them in and out, use more rubbing varnish and finishing varnish than is put on any other surrey manufactured. The body panels are jet black; the seat panels and seat backs are finished with a rich Brewster green, which harmonizes beautifully with the black body; the pillars are painted a dark blood carmine. The gear, wheels and shafts are painted a rich Brewster green, neatly striped with a double line of glazed carmine. The entire effect of the painting on this job makes it very attractive. Can furnish blood carmine gear if ordered.

TRACK. 4 feet 8 inches or 5 feet 2 inches. State width wanted. Net weight, about 575 pounds.

$93.95

No. 11K1442	Price, complete with extension top, double braced shafts and steel tires	$93.95
No. 11K1444	Price, complete with extension top, double braced shafts and cut under body	$97.75
No. 11K1342	Price, complete with canopy top in place of extension top	87.95
No. 11K1344	Price, complete with canopy top in place of extension top and cut under style body	92.45

EXTRAS

Pole in place of shafts		2.00
Both pole and shafts		4.90
1-inch Kelly Springfield guaranteed rubber tires		17.85

Shipping weight, crated under 50 inches, about 770 pounds. Shipped from factory.

The 1908 Sears & Roebuck huge mail catalogue listed this page of selections of surreys. Elegant colors were offered. Black and rich Brewster green trimmed in dark carmine.

— *Author's Collection*

Harper's Bazar for Jan. 14, 1882, used this drawing on its front cover. Bundled in warm clothing and covered with lap robes, the travellers tried to stay warm. Umbrellas helped fend off the driving snow.

— *Author's Collection*

Chapter Six

Winter Problems

In the Northern regions of the United States, snow in the winter months was inevitable — so ways were devised to live with it.

Generally, after a storm the snow rollers were brought out to pack down the white stuff and make the roads beautiful for sleigh runners. Salting, sanding and scraping bare was unthinkable.

Merchants used sleighs for deliveries. Sleigh runners fitted with hubs to slide over axle ends on buggies or delivery wagons were available. The wheels were simply removed and the sleigh runners slipped on.

Some towns maintained Snow Wardens whose job it was to see that roads and streets had no bare spots where the wind had blown away the falling snow. Such spots had snow scraped over to cover and then packed with a roller. The same was true with covered bridges. Snow had to be dragged in and packed.

On cold winter days, every man who had any consideration for his horses would always warm the bit by holding it in his hand or blowing his warm breath on it. An ice-cold steel bit could tear the tender skin on the horse's mouth.

Equipping horse shoes with caulks was another winter task. Horses were particularly vulnerable if icy conditions were encountered.

Some towns had ordinances requiring the use of sleigh bells as this was the only way a fast-moving horse and cutter could be heard as it slipped silently along the well-packed snow.

In 1886, this print appeared in Harper's Weekly. An accompanying story said "...the general public travelling afoot or on wheels has been gaping in open-mouthed astonishment at the interminable procession of jingling, shiny, gorgeous things passing in and out of Central Park.

— *Author's Collection*

Ten horses struggle to pull a rig that is brushing snow off the railway tracks in New York City. This print appeared in a January, 1887, issue of Harper's Weekly.

— *Author's Collection*

In the northern tiers of states where heavy snowfalls were commonplace, it was more expedient to pack down the snow than try to remove it. To this end, communities used horse drawn snow rollers. Well-packed snow was an excellent base for the myriad of sleighs in use. This snow roller was in use in Bethel, Vt., in 1915.

— *Frank Woodward Collection*

A January 1918 blizzard left Milwaukee streets untenable for auto traffic but a horse drawn cutter seen in the distance had no problems navigating the deep snow.

— *Milwaukee Public Museum*

Left: As late as 1940, when this photo was taken, Milwaukee found it more economical to plow sidewalks in parks and public facilities with a team of horses.

— *Author's Photo*

Below: A heavy snow has caused a foul-up of traffic on South Street in New York. A delivery wagon on the sidewalk seems to be teetering; perhaps caused by a broken wheel. The five-horse team and the four-horse team appear to have very heavy loads for these street conditions.

— *Motor Vehicle Manufacturer's Assoc.*

The horses seem to be having a difficult time with their heavily loaded wagon. Unless properly shod with caulks, the horses did not have any grip and a slight upgrade, as shown here, made it miserable for them. Note nosebags hanging on the corner of the wagon.

— *Motor Vehicle Manufacturer's Assoc.*

The article in Leslies Illustrated News (1865) says of this drawing "We can almost hear the old lady tell her husband not to let the team get ahead."

— *Author's Collection*

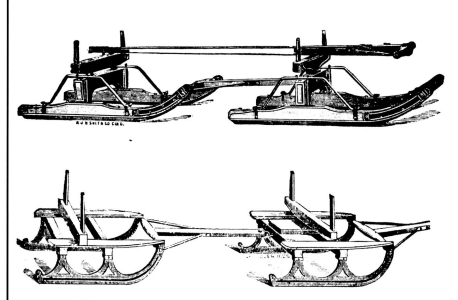

Sleigh runners of all sizes were available from various manufacturers. Standard wagon boxes would fit between the bolsters.

— Author's Collection

The Hudson River at Albany, New York, became a thoroughfare in winter. This 1853 illustration shows public conveyance, merchandise vehicles and pedestrians all using the frozen river.

— Author's Collection

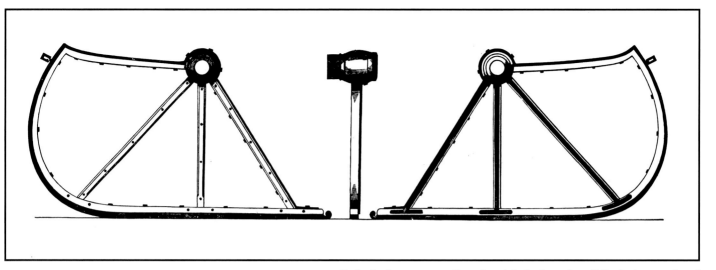

Bobsled runners fitted with hubs simplified the task of equipping a vehicle for winter use.

Most lightweight buggys and delivery wagons had standard sized tapered axles, thus could be equipped easily with a set of runners.

— *Author's Collection*

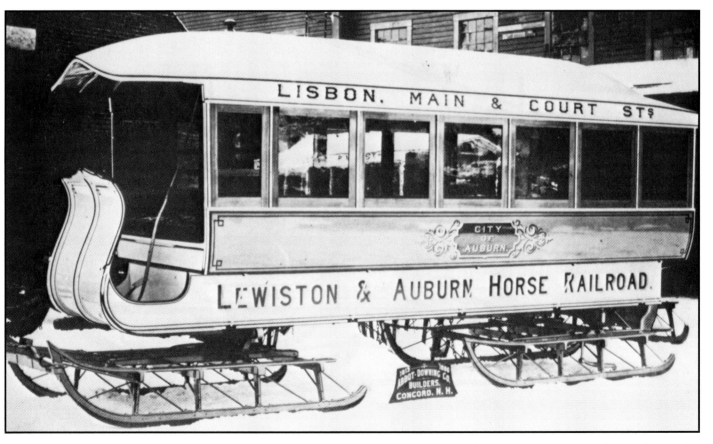

Some northern cities found it impossible to keep the tracks used by horse drawn street cars free of clogging and freezing snow and ice. They resorted to omnibuses equipped with bobsled runners.

— *Smithsonian Institution*

Milk deliveries continued in spite of the deep snow. This 1931 scene was photographed in St. Paul, Minn.

— *Philip Weber Collection*

Opposite: The raging blizzard had downed a live power line which electrocuted the horse on which it fell. The artist, Max Klepper, has caught the bitterness of the Boston storm and the tragedy of the situation in his 1898 drawing.

— *Author's Collection*

A matched pair of black horses drew this hearse equipped with bobsled runners for winter use.

— *Schenectady (N.Y.) Gazette*

A street scene in Lowville, New York, in the 1880's shows bobsled loads of firewood waiting to unload. Two empty sleds on right have accomplished their unloading. Howell's Hotel omnibus is parked and ready for a trip to the depot.

— Ron Ryder Collection

Blustery, snowy weather did not stop mail delivery on the Rural Free Delivery routes.

— U.S. Postal Service

A travelling peddler from New Hampshire had Downing & Sons produce this handsome outfit. C. 1860.

Scenery painted on the sides gave the rig a good-looking appearance.

— *New Hampshire Historical Society*

Chapter Seven

Distinctive Vehicles

The vehicle manufacturers produced an astounding array of carts, buggys, carriages and wagons to meet just about any demand or whim.

In addition, there were a variety of vehicles that were produced by only certain manufacturers that were used in limited quantities because of their distinctive use.

A few of these specialized horse drawn vehicles are illustrated in this chapter.

In some instances, a standard wagon was purchased and then modified to fit the specific requirements of the industry.

Hearses and pop corn wagons are examples of very specialized horse drawn conveyances. The features required by their uses were so restricted that, in the overall picture, there were very few producers of such equipage.

Peddler's wagons had special requirements. These itinerant salesmen travelled the countryside and went from farm to farm and door to door in small towns. Their wagons on the outside looked rather normal, but the interiors were very special with built-in compartments, sliding trays and cubbyholes. Every bit of available space had a hinged door. Frequently, the roof was equipped with a railing on which bulky merchandise could be carried. A hinged rack on the rear of the vehicle was used for boxes of goods.

Some special vehicles were equipped with winches. Others, with under-slung axles bringing the body low to the road.

Occasionally, some very distinct wagon bodies were produced primarily for advertising purposes. An example was H.J. Heinz Company's rig with a body shaped like a pickle jar.

Novel designs for delivery of products were those shaped like cigars, or a globe if the company happened to be the Globe Products.

Many such vehicles were strictly for advertising and promotions. Others were, in addition, practical and conspicuous delivery vehicles.

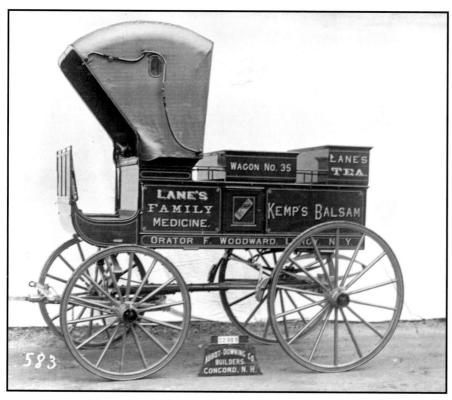

Left: "Wagon No. 35" painted on the side would indicate the owner had a string of these medicine peddlers on the road. C. 1885.

Hinged doors opened to various compartments where products were carried.

— *New Hampshire Historical Society*

Below: An Iowa scene in 1911. This couple started in business in a modest way with this popcorn wagon.

— *Philip Weber Collection*

In about 1915, the DeKalb (Ill.) Wagon Company's catalogue illustrated a special wagon for hauling pianos and organs. The body was 9' 6" long, 37" wide. Depending on the model, the vehicle could haul loads up to 1,500 pounds. The body could be finished in green, black, yellow, or red, with the undergear red or yellow.

— *Author's Collection*

Philadelphia Railway Transit Co. developed this very specialized service wagon for repairing overhead trolley wires. The platform could be cranked up to a height that made the wires accessible to the workmen on the platform.

— *Philip Weber Collection*

An 1885 scene. A mounted policeman clears the road as he gallops ahead of the ambulance rushing to an accident scene.

— *Author's Collection*

The Boston Fire Department provided a horse ambulance service. With hundreds of horses working the city streets, there were occasional accidents. In some instances, aged horses could not stand the summer's heat.

— *Bill Noonan Collection*

Hearses were painted black and were generally highly decorated with wood-carved trimmings. This team lacks the stylishness in conformation and harness usually found on this type of conveyance.

— *Sauk County (Wis.) Historical Society*

The rather small white hearse indicates the funeral was for a child. The cortege lines up for a photo in 1913 in Schnectady, New York.

— *Schenectady Gazette*

DEKALB WAGON COMPANY

The New Way

The Old Way

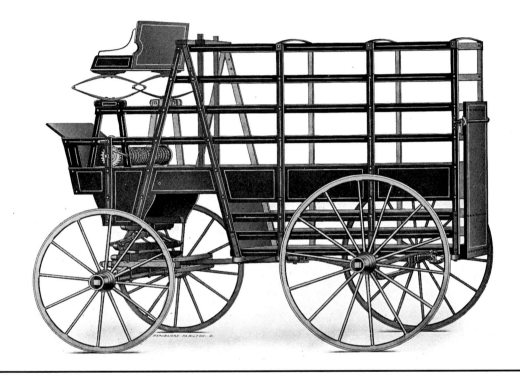

The body of this livestock wagon is designed to carry a horse or cow as well as hogs, sheep, or calves. It had a capacity of a one ton load. C. 1915.

— *Author's Collection*

A standard wagon body was made into a school bus. Note the seats running lengthwise, rolled up side curtains and rear step.

— *Norm Coughlin Collection*

A 1908 ambulance in Cleveland, Ohio. Note the bell under the footboard. This ambulance was equipped with hard rubber tires on the wheels.

— *Cleveland Public Library*

The casket wagon was available with or without the beveled plate glass side panels. It was furnished as an all black vehicle. If gray or white was preferred, there was an extra charge.

— *Author's Collection*

The Milwaukee Hospital provided ambulance service in 1913. Note the large carriage lamps required for night service.

— *Milwaukee Public Library*

Commonwealth Edison, Co. of Chicago reworked a wagon to fit their special needs. Note the racks with hooks, bins (with cover in up position) and sliding drawer.

— *Philip Weber Collection*

— *Percheron Horse Association*

Chapter Eight

The Horses

"One white foot - buy him

Two white feet - try him

Three white feet - deny him

Four white feet - throw him to the crows."

This interesting couplet appeared in the Aug. 16, 1899 issue of the Breeders Gazette.

The same magazine six years earlier had an article that discussed the type of draft horse most desirable for New York City:

"Preferably, the horses should not weigh over 1,600 pounds for the general trucking business. They should be clean-limbed, flat-boned and with good feet as the paved streets and car tracks play havoc on the horses when they carry too much flesh. The long-legged, heavy horses becomes banged up in no time.

"Horses five to six years old weighing from 1,350 to 1,550 pounds, not too much daylight under them, active movers, short backs, good depth through the heart, on the Percheron type would find a ready market at prices from $500 to $700 at team. It is hard today to find such a team.

"The overgrown horse over 1,700 pounds is of no account with us. It will always prove to the advantage of horsemen to have their horses broken single and double and not hog fat."

By 1920, the picture was changing. Wayne Dinsmore, Secretary of the Horse Association of America wrote in the Breeder's Gazette:

"The heavy draft horse has not suffered particularly in the estimation of the cartage and transfer companies. The Willett Teaming Co. of Chicago noted that they introduced 3,400 pound teams instead of 2,600 pound teams; 10,000 pound ball–bearing double wagons instead of 6,000 pound wagons; the wheels underneath wide bed wagons for light and bulky freight (these wagons haul six pianos instead of three); ball bearing, three horse wagons loading normally 16,000 pounds to replace the old four horse team which normally loaded 13,000 pounds.

"The Chapman Lumber Co. of Syracuse, New York, recently purchased a 3,600 pound pair of matched grade Belgian mares for $1,200.

"'After studying the matter carefully, we bought these mares not for show or advertising purposes but as a cold hard business investment. We consider them the best power hauling unit that we ever owned.'

"J.M. Horton Ice Cream Co. of New York uses 350 horses and 60 motor trucks. 'The horses cover all stops within a radius of 10 miles from the plant. Our teams cover between 15 and 20 miles and make 35 to 40 stops. We can run a two-horse rig at a cost of $15 a day including driver's wages. It costs us $25 a day to operate a truck.'"

This livestock journal frequently ran stories like these. The efficiency of the horse for city work was difficult to dispute. Even so, with the gradual increase of motorized traffic, and the greater traffic speeds, the demise of horse drawn rigs was inevitable.

Salvador and Lescout were champions on the fair circuit during the era of 1900. Artist George Ford Morris drew these fine Percherons. The Percheron breed was developed in France. They are grey or black in color.

— Anna Fox Collection

Left: Clydesdale type at the turn of the century — Stallion Sindar (4714). This breed was developed in Scotland. The colors are bay, brown or black and much white on face and legs.

— *Anna Fox Collection*

Below: Suffolk Punch Stallion. Solid chestnut in color, this breed originated in the County of Suffolk in England.

— *Richard Hemphill Collection*

Classy action of this chestnut Hackney stallion is obvious in George Ford Morris' 1905 painting.

— Anna Fox Collection

Champion Heavy Harness pair Lord Golden and Lord Brilliant in 1902.

— Anna Fox Collection

The Morgan horse was stylish in appearance and used frequently in harness. The foundation of this breed was a remarkable stallion, Justin Morgan, who was about 14 hands and weighed about 950 pounds, dark bay, with black mane and tail. This stallion died in 1821 but the breed has remained the most popular American-bred, general-purpose horse.

— Anna Fox Collection

A light spider phaeton with basket seat and rumble with English canopy presents very smart and fashionable equipage.

— Anna Fox Collection

A splendid demonstration of driving in this 1910 photo. Mr. John Goodwin is presenting this random hitch.

— Anna Fox Collection

A German Coach Stallion was painted in 1904 by George Ford Morris.

— *Anna Fox Collection*

George Ford Morris caught the magnificent action of this French Coach Stallion in his 1904 painting.

— *Anna Fox Collection*

Above: Many horse importers used postcards to advertise. A picture of their operation was impressive. This card shows Truman's Pioneer Stud Farm at Bushnell, Illinois.

— *Author's Collection*

Below: A four story stable is indeed an oddity. All the stalls appear filled in this, the world's only horse hotel in Charlottenburg, Germany.

— *Anna Fox Collection*

Carnot developed into one of the greatest sires of all time, winning championships in classes at the Chicago International, New York Horse Show, Wisconsin State Fair, Illinois State Fair and Indiana State Fair. This picture was taken in 1909 before his importation by J. Crouch of Lafayette, Ind.

— *Author's Collection*

In 1926, the Fisk Tire Company ran a series of ads in major magazines.

— *Author's Collection*

Chapter Nine

The Mules

A mule is the result of breeding a donkey to a horse. The resulting hybrid, the mule, is almost always sterile and incapable of reproducing itself.

"The American mule is superior to the mule of any other country" according to the Standard Jack and Jennet Registry of America. "This superiority is attributed to an abundance of proper food and the use of better mares for breeding. The natural consequence was the production of the typical American Draft Mule.

"The U.S. Army Quartermaster General was quoted as saying that there was no comparison between the small, poorly nourished mule obtained in Spain and southern France and the powerful upstanding mule of the middle west of America."

The Registry sums up their belief in the mule by saying "The mule has greater strength in proportion to its size; has more endurance; is more active and sure footed; requires less food; is longer-lived and less susceptible to disease than any other beast of burden.

"The Mule can endure both heat and cold better than the horse. He has greater instinct of self preservation and will refrain from over-eating. In short, he is possessed of more of the essentials of an ideal beast of burden than is any other animal."

The U.S. Army had a high regard for the mule. During World War I, thousands upon thousands of big midwestern mules were used by the army and more thousands were shipped to our Allies.

A manual published by the U.S. Army and written by Col. Phillip Booker stated "A mule will not pull more, weight for weight, than a horse. Mules are considered to have a better brain and reasoning power than horses. Mules are equally tractable if handled with patience and kindness.

"Horses, if given the opportunity, will over-eat. Mules, on the other hand, seldom over-eat. Mules are not as tractable in harness as horses. While their pulling power is equal, they cannot be manipulated and handled as horses. Mules are much more inclined to take matters into their own hands. They were never adopted universally for artillery teams. They do not lend themselves to the postillion method of driving.

"For wagon transportation where the teamster is mounted on a seat of the wagon and controls the animals through the use of lines, mules are about as tractable as horses.

"Mules will herd, that is, follow a leader far better than horses. This instinct makes them more suitable for pack units. Pack mules, properly trained, will follow a bell leader over any terrain, if they can get through. The average pack mule will carry a payload of about 210 pounds. The Phillips pack saddle, both cargo and cavalry type, provides the best equipment. Once adjusted, it remains intact and can be fitted to any type of mule. The girth must be kept tight at all times. The loads must be balanced — an equal weight on each side of the saddle."

About forty miles north of Kansas City, Missouri, two cousins, J.D. Guyton and W.R. Harrington, developed an enormously successful Mule Company in the first two decades of the Twentieth Century. Their headquarters was in Lathrop. In their vast operation, the three principal mule barns housed 1,000 animals in each. It took 500 buyers spanning the countryside to keep up with the demand.

The Guyton and Harrington Mule Company secured an exclusive contract with the British War Office. They started by supplying the British during the Boer War and, later, during World War I. In 1914, the they handled over 130,000 mules and horses.

The mule has earned a prominent place in the overall picture of draft animals in America .

One of the most unusual jobs the mule was called upon to get done was towing canal boats and barges. They were the predominate source of power in moving the powerless boats.

A boy would ride and care for the mules. The team had a steady pull on the 100-foot tow rope as it trudged along the tow path moving its floating load, the barge. Mules seemed to be best for this kind of work. This 1915 scene is on the Delaware Canal in Pennsylvania.

— *Hugh Moore Historic Museum*

Lock No. 70 near Boonville, New York, on the Black RIver Canal which connected with the Erie Canal in Rome, New York. The mule team is resting while the barge it is towing is being lowered. The barges carried passengers and/or cargo.

— *Ron Ryder Collection*

Loads of raw cotton all drawn by mules wait in line to unload where the product will be baled.

— *Tennessee State Museum*

See page 218 for the story of the famous 20-Mule-Teams that hauled Borax through Death Valley during the 1880s.

A team of six mules patiently await the loading or unloading of the wagon along the New Orleans levee.

— *Henry Ford Museum*

Mule teams bring loads of sugar cane in from the fields at this Louisiana Sugar Mill.

— *Henry Ford Museum*

7th ANNUAL SALE—50 JACKS and JENNETS—50

AT THE

Lafayette County Jack Farm

Adjoining HIGGINSVILLE, MO.,

on main line of C. & A. and Sedalia Branch of
Missouri Pacific, 55 miles east of Kansas City,

TUESDAY, MARCH 2

25 head of High-Class Registered Jacks
and 25 head of Registered Jennets.

Every animal registered and guaranteed
as represented. Among the jacks are
Hayes McChord, five years old, stands
15½ hands, a son of Dr. McChord, and is
a great prizewinner. Other great speci-
mens are Dr. Long Jr., a son of Dr. Long,
which sold for $2,500. 4 high-class jacks
by Dr. Long, 5 by Dr. McChord, 6 by
Expansion and 3 by St. Patrick, and these
jacks and others are the very best I have
ever sold publicly or privately. They have
perfect markings, are heavy-boned and
are high-class herd jacks. More of the
Dr. McChord breeding than I have ever
sold before. The jennets include 20 head
that are showing in foal to Dr. Shields,
that sold for $2,000—the big smooth kind
with lots of bone and quality. There is
not an undesirable jennet in this sale.

WRITE FOR THE CATALOG,
mentioning The Breeder's Gazette.
P. M. GROSS, AUCTIONEER.

THE KIND OF JACKS AND JENNETS INCLUDED IN THIS SALE.

W. J. FINLEY, Higginsville, Mo.

THE SIXTH ANNUAL SALE

OF THE

Clover Leaf Valley Jack Farm

AT LA PLATA, MO.

Will be given on MARCH 8, 1915.

This sale will be given in the largest exclusive Jack and
Jennet Sale Pavilion in the United States. 24 passenger
trains stop at La Plata each day. Pavilion situated 100
yards from depots. **25 head of the highest class
registered jacks** ever offered in any sale. **25 jennets** of the very best conformation and breeding in
America, many of them with colts by their side.

THE BLOODLINES OF MAMMOTH J. C. 2046, ORPHAN BOY 696, LIMESTONE MAMMOTH 298
and many other of the greatest jacks in the world will be sold both in jacks and jennets.

THE GREATEST COLLECTION OF JACKS AND JENNETS TO BE OFFERED IN 1915.

IN YOU ARE INTERESTED IN JACKS OR JENNETS WRITE FOR THE GREATEST CATALOG
OF THIS STOCK EVER PRINTED, showing the photograph of each animal and giving the
extended pedigree. I SELL MORE HIGH-CLASS JACKS THAT PAY FOR THEMSELVES IN
ONE YEAR THAN ANY MAN IN AMERICA. Address

G. C. ROAN, Proprietor, LA PLATA, MACON CO., MO.

SIGLER & SHANNON'S

Jack and Jennet Sale

25 JACKS, 10 JENNETS.

*A great lot; the big black kind, 15 to 16 hands, with big
bone and big head and ears.*

The blood of Limestone Mammoth, High Ball, Starlight, Pharaoh, Paragon, Brignolia and Taxpayer
will predominate in this offering. Sale held in heated pavilion regardless of weather at

Greencastle, Indiana, March 4

Best of railroad accommodations from all points. We assure critical jack buyers that they will not
be disappointed in attending this sale, as the stock consists of a very high-class lot. For illustrated
catalog address, mentioning The Breeder's Gazette,

J. O. SIGLER, Greencastle, Indiana, or   CHAS. B. SHANNON, Russellville, Indiana.

Harriman, West, Burks, Sayler Bros. and Potter, Auctioneers.

THIRD ANNUAL SALE

Wednesday, Feb. 24,   Cape Girardeau, Mo.

20 HEAD OF JACKS AND JENNETS

Jacks from weanlings to six years old. All two years and up, 15 to 16 hands standard measure.
Some have 34½-inch ear and weigh close to 1,100 lbs. Everything guaranteed as represented.
Write for Catalog, mentioning The Breeder's Gazette.

BEN M. GREEN, CAPE GIRARDEAU, CAPE GIRARDEAU COUNTY, MISSOURI.

PUBLIC SALE.

Sixth Annual Sale of 15 head of High-Class Registered

BLACK JACKS

and 25 head of registered POLAND-CHINA HOGS, consisting of Bred Gilts and Young Boars,

JACKSON, MO., TUESDAY, FEB. 23.

Sale will take place at my barn, under big tent which will be supplied
with comfortable seats and heaters. These jacks are all in good enough flesh to begin the season
with, ranging in age from 2 to 6 years, from 14¾ to 15¾ hands standard measure. They are the big-
boned kind, that will appeal to anyone looking for a high-class jack to use either on mares or jennets. Every animal guaranteed as represented. If inter-
ested write for catalog, mentioning Breeder's Gazette   W. F. SCHADE, Jackson, Mo.

World War I caused a tremendous
demand for mules. In the February
11, 1915, issue of the Breeder's
Gazette, these ads offered Jacks
without which no mules would be
produced.

— *Author's Collection*

160

Beautifully matched spans were first prize winners at the 1915 Iowa State Fair for their owner Wyatt Carr of Collins, Iowa.

— *Author's Collection*

Loading shocks of wheat on an Iowa farm. The mules will take the load to the thresher in the distance.

— *Milwaukee Public Museum*

Two four-mule teams ae drawing two-bottom gang plows. They turned six acres a day. The farm was located in Mason County, Illinois. C. 1926.

— *Author's Collection*

Mule power moves this grain combine and with the family all proudly looking on, this might have been a new acquisition.

— *Philip Weber Collection*

Four tough, well-broken mules prepare to add their power to assist a truck that had slithered off the road in France.

— *National Archives*

World War I photo of an ammunition wagon northeast of St. Michiel, France. The going is uphill, slippery and muddy for the mules.

— *National Archives*

A convoy of mule drawn wagons in 1932. About a decade later mules and horses were no longer in the service.

— John Conners Collection

Artillerymen with loaded pack mules. The sure-footed animals could carry loads up to 300 pounds. The U.S. Army felt that, because of their shorter back and lower withers, the mule made a better pack animal than the horse.

— U.S. Army

In World War I, 20,000 mules served with the U.S. Army in Europe. Tens of thousands more were shipped to our allies. Photo shows a mule depot.

— *National Archives*

The U.S. Army used mules for years. Here is a six mule hitch with a jerk line. This type of equipment passed from the scene years ago.

— *U.S. Army Transportation Museum*

Not the latest style, perhaps, but the bonnets did ward off the hot sun on a severely hot day.

— *Philip Weber Collection*

Chapter Ten

Maintaining the Horses

In 1896, the Baltimore Sun carried an interesting piece on the White House stables. The story said Presidents Harrison (1889-1893) and Cleveland (1885-1889 and 1893-1897) maintained more extensive stables of horses than any other President.

"Gen. Harrison had four equipages and six horses — the best from Kentucky.

"President Cleveland is the first to have a sleigh. During the cold season, he frequently joined the parades on the main thoroughfares.

"Carriages are all glistening black with no ornaments except his initials 'G.C.' on the doors and on the silver on the harness.

"Stables are in the rear of the White House about 400 yards distant.

"The President's livery is handsome and simple. A dark green coat with trousers to match and a high hat without cockade or ornamentation. None of the coachmen wear trousers fitted skin tight to the legs.

"The footman is dressed in accordance with prevailing styles and has his lower extremities encased in linen duck. His coat and hat match those of the coachman."

Stables were a very important part of maintaining horses —clean, dry and airy (but no drafts), were basic requirements.

Also important was caring for the feet. "No foot, no horse," said Ellis McFarland, secretary of the Percheron Horse Association in 1936.

Every hamlet, village, town or city had blacksmith shops. Horse Shoeing was important. A nostalgic article on the subject was written by Loren Osman, Farm Editor of the Milwaukee Journal in 1957. Excerpts from this story are reprinted on page 182.

Caring for harness properly seemed to be a neglected chore. In 1893, the American Agriculturist Magazine chastised farmers and gave a few hints for the proper maintenance of harness.

"It is not a rare sight to see a farmer's heavy draft harness that has been used for several years without a drop of any lubricant touching them since they came from the dealer's hands. All the leather portion is hard and brittle and presents a dull appearance.

"Before oiling harness, remove all dirt and dandruff by thoroughly washing with strong castile soap. As soon as dry, any of the harness oils may be applied with a woolen cloth or soft sponge, using care to saturate every portion. After each strap has been oiled, bend it back and forth, thereby introducing the oil to the very center of each strap.

"In place of the usual neat's foot oil or petroleum harness oil, melted lard, free of salt, or even unsalted butter may be used. It is better still to boil up the broken shin bones of a beef. The marrow and what tallow there may be will make a most valuable dressing of almost the consistency of oil and may be bottled for future use. If color be desired, add a little lampblack."

Feeding of horses was important. What was fed and the amount was determined by the weight of the horse, his condition and the work he did. Articles in the agriculture papers regularly and frequently quoted the stable bosses of the big companies that had hundreds of drafters.

For example, in the July 5, 1899, Breeder's Gazette, an article on "Feed for City Draft Horses" gave some interesting figures for the feed requirements of 1,400 to 1,500 pound drafters.

Swift, Armour and American Railway Express fed 16 to 18 pounds of oats and 16 to 20 pounds of hay per day. Armour cut back a few pounds a day on hay because they fed four ears of corn daily. Usually on one weekend day the horses were fed lightly and given a bran and oat mash.

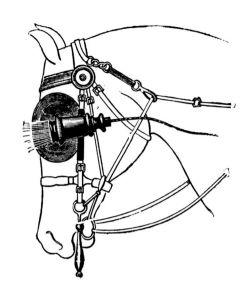

FIG. 1.—BLINDER LAMPS.

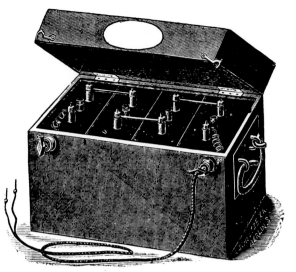

FIG. 3.—STORAGE BATTERIES.

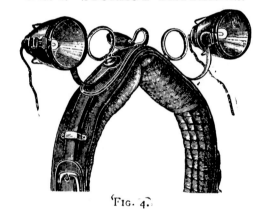

FIG. 4.

FIG. 4.—LAMPS FOR FOUR-IN-HAND TEAMS.

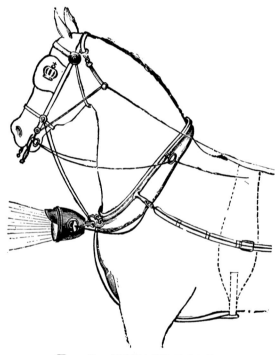

FIG. 2.—BREAST LAMP.

FIG. 5.—POLE LAMP.

Electric Lights for horses were illustrated in the Jan. 26, 1895, issue of Scientific American Supplement. To a certain extent, such equipment was used in Europe, but was never prevalent in America.

— Author's Collection

Most cities and towns provided watering troughs for horses. Elaborate fountains like this one in Kilbourn (now Wisconsin Dells), Wis., were not too common. The cups at the base were for dogs. Horses used the two large tanks. The small receptacles beneath the fish heads provided a stream for people. Birds drank from the bowl in the statue's hand. C. 1890.

— *H. H. Bennett Studios*

Hitching posts, being a necessity, were very common along the streets. Some were wooden posts decoratively turned as shown. Other posts had attractive cast-iron horse heads. Still others were stone or concrete. Steel rings to which the horse was tied were attached to the tops of such hitching posts.

— *Milwaukee Public Library*

This handsome watering trough stood in the intersection of two streets in front of Milwaukee's City Hall. The bronze statue and fountain were dedicated to Henry Bergh in 1891. Mr. Bergh was the founder of the American Society for the Prevention of Cruelty to Animals.

— *Milwaukee Public Library*

As late as 1940, Sears, Roebuck & Co. offered a variety of styles of harness.

— Sears, Roebuck & Co.

A shake of the horse's head, and the dangling leather tassels kept the flies away.

— *Anheuser - Busch Co.*

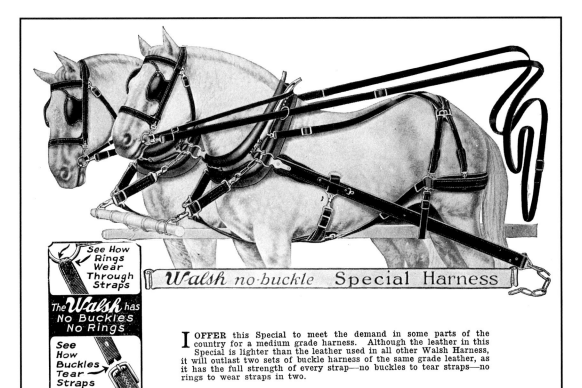

In 1926, the Walsh Harness Co. of Milwaukee was listing special "no-buckle" harnesses.

— *Author's Collection*

The fly net was for the horse's comfort. It discouraged insects that the horse could not reach with a swish of his tail. C. 1905.

— Robert Chandler Collection

Use high quality Fly Nets for your Horses

Osnaburg Covers

Give your horses good protection with these Osnaburg Covers. Light in weight, but strong and sturdy in construction. Made of high quality white fabric. Covers have leather trimmed hame and terret openings, bound ear holes, and web trace loops. Buy covers for your horses at Sears low price.

$1.18 Each 100-inch

10 E 844—100-inch length. Shipping weight, 1 lb. 4 oz.... Each .$1.18
10 E 845—110-inch length. Shipping weight, 1 lb. 8 oz.... Each. $1.28

Belting-leather Fly Nets

Increase the working efficiency of your horses and mules by using these serviceable Fly Nets. Big full-sized nets, made from belting leather ... built on a framework of ½-inch leather bars. 60 leather lashes, 7 feet long, are stapled to the leather bar framework. Lashes also stapled to front piece. Buckle-front fastener. You'll like these durable leather nets for your animals. Shipping weight, 4 pounds 8 ounces.

$1.95 Each

10 E 816................Each $1.95

Open-weave Duck Covers

A combination style fly cover made of open weave hose duck, tan color. The weave is open enough to keep animals cool, yet closely enough woven to keep out the smallest flies. Ear holes strongly reinforced. Leather trimmed hame and terret openings, and leather trimmed openings for lines. Front and back edges turned, stitched. 50 lashes stitched to bottom.

$1.92 100-inch

10 E 828-100 in. Shpg. wt., 2 lbs.. $1.92
10 E 829—110 in. Shipping wt., 2 pounds 4 ounces...........$2.03

Black Cord Nets

Made of high quality tightly twisted 3-ply black waterproofed cotton cords, metal tipped. Lashes are about 7½ feet long woven through five 4-strand braided bars, 62 inches long. Breast piece has 24 lashes. Snap-and-ring fastener.

$2.88 Each 60-Lashes

Number of Lashes	Catalog number	Shipping weight	Price Each
60	10 E 818	3 lbs. 8 oz.	$2.88
70	10 E 819	3 lbs. 12 oz.	3.15
84	10 E 820	4 lbs.	3.39
100	10 E 821	4 lbs. 10 oz.	3.89

Sears, Roebuck & Co. offered this line of fly nets.

— Author's Collection

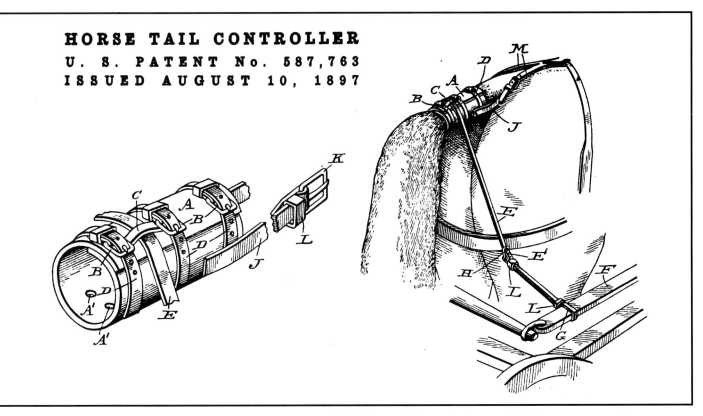

This ignominious device probably never caught on as no advertisements or photographs of it have ever shown up.

— *Anna Fox Collection*

Horses in city delivery work were fed their standard ration at noon. Canvas nose bags or sometimes pails were used. The near horse is resting its bag on the wagon pole. This enabled it to reach every last bit of grain.

— *Philip Weber Collection*

A carriage house and stable at the rear of the home made for a convenient set up for those well-to-do people. Living quarters for the groom and coachman were usually included. Those who owned horses for riding or driving and did not have stable facilities boarded their horses at a livery stable. The home and stable shown was the residence of R.P. Howell in Racine, Wis. C. 1890.

— *Racine County Historical Society*

The more palatial homes not only had stables in the rear, but they usually had a port cochere included which was equipped with a high step. This made it easy for people to step from the porch to carriage. In this photo of the Al Ringling mansion in Baraboo, Wis., the port cochere is seen.

— *Author's Photo*

Some companies that had a large enough complement of horses had a staff veterinarian. Others who owned horses used an independent vet of which there were always plenty. In this photo of the stable of American Steel & Wire Co., a vet works while an attendent holds the drafter with a twitch on its nose.

— *Philip Weber Collection*

The neat, well-kept stable of John D. Rockefeller at Pocantico Hills, New York.

— *Author's Collection*

Most large companies that stabled 200 or 300 or more horses included a special building in their complex. This was the stable facility of the Pabst Brewing Co. in Milwaukee.

— *Author's Collection*

Left: Typical horse barn of a small farmer. No barn boys to keep things clean, so the farmer did this chore once a day.

— *Author's Photo*

Below: Some dealers in horse and stable furnishings offered braided straw matting for floors and stall posts. "Mats, pilicans, crowns and rosettes could be furnished in colored braids to suit all tastes."

— *Tom Ryder Collection*

The 1910 blacksmith shop in Boonville, New York. William Baker operated the establishment and was known for miles around. Like all blacksmith shops, it was a gathering place for getting the latest information and gossip as well as spreading the same. Mr. Baker was also the Village Mayor, so his shop was a particularly good spot to visit and get the latest news.

— *Ron Ryder Collection*

The Neighborhood Blacksmith

"The season's first big snowfall never fails to bring a line of motorists to filling stations and garages, clamoring for snow tires and chains. Turn back half a century and you have almost the same scene: Just substitute horses for automobiles, blacksmiths for garage men, and sharp pointed horse shoes for chains and snow tires.

When a group of old-time blacksmiths got together a few years ago in Milwaukee, one of them recalled that in the annual winter rush for nonskid equipment for slipping teams, as many as 50 horses were shod in a single day. One blacksmith stayed on the job for 23 hours, swinging a four-pound hammer.

A whole generation has grown up without the opportunity of seeing a horse being shod. The ring of the blacksmith's hammer and anvil is seldom heard in villages these days. Children no longer huddle in the doorway of the sooty shop, watch the sparks fly from the forge and hear the moan of the hand-cranked bellows. They have never sniffed the unforgettable odor of a horse's hoof scorched by red hot iron as the smith tried on a shoe for size. And they have never worn a ring, fashioned from a horseshoe nail with a hammer which looked so clumsy, yet could do such delicate work.

Henry Wadsworth Longfellow was the blacksmith's greatest press agent. The poet made the chestnut tree as much a part of the setting for the smithy as the blacksmith himself.

The smith's anvil, mounted on a chunk of oak, lasted him a lifetime. On it he mended broken carriage parts and sleighs and fashioned ornamental ironwork. But horseshoeing was his main line of work and the one for which the blacksmith is most fondly remembered.

Typical anvil sitting on a solid block of wood was the work bench of any smithy.

— *Gene Baxter Collection*

Short or tall, the smith had to be muscular, and he displayed his brawn by seldom wearing a shirt. Under his leather apron and greasy pants, he wore long underwear, winter or summer.

The smith was a man of courage as well as strength. He would walk up to a strange horse, lift its foot and begin his work. The hoof had to be cleaned and pared with a sharp knife, drawshave and rasp before the shoe could be fitted. An un-cooperative horse was subdued with a nose twitch, or, in extreme cases, hoisted on a belly band or thrown to the floor.

The smith in early times had to fashion shoes out of blank metal. Later, partly fabricated shoes were available and were hung on long pegs in the shop. After the shoe was shaped, nails were driven slantwise through it and the hoof, then were snipped off at the top with long pincers and clinched.

The romantic setting of the blacksmith was hard to beat. In one corner of the gloomy shop was the heap of glowing coals, from which the smith, his face lit by the fire, would pull searing hunks of metal. Sparks would fly as he pounded the rapidly graying metal into shape on his anvil.

There was a hiss of steam as he plunged the hot metal into a rain barrel, to cool. The smith then would wait for the rainbow bands of color that guided him in "tempering."

The fitting of iron rims on wagon and carriage wheels also was a big portion of the business. After the tire had been shaped, it was fitted hot, then shrunk onto the wheel by plunging the whole thing into a (water) tank.

The blacksmith's shop was the social center of its day. It was a real he-man's club, where jokes and tall tales were exchanged along with comments on the weather, politics, and how best to handle a lively mare.

"A man," said one of the oldtime blacksmiths, "really took care of his horses in those days." A well-traveled horse was reshod every six weeks. The normal charge was 30¢ to shoe a draft horse and 15¢ to reset shoes.

— *Loren Osman*
Milwaukee Journal

The village smithy usually had a messy shop due to the nature of the business. The odors of burning hooves, manure, sweating horses, coal gas from the forge, tobacco juice spat here and there, all added to the romance of these great spots made famous by Longfellow's memorable poem "The Village Blacksmith."

— *Ron Ryder Collection*

An 1888 advertise-
ment for Putnam horse
shoe nails.

— *Author's Collection*

In winter, with ice and snowy conditions, most horses were sharp-shod to keep them from slipping. Calks came in a variety of shapes, each for a different condition. The Fruin Drop Forge Co. circulated this card to potential customers.

— *Author's Collection*

Dan Patch was an unusually tractable horse. When racing, his bridle never had blinders and always a simple bit was used. In retirement, as seen here, the great pacer was enjoyed by the children for sleigh riding.

— *Anna Fox Collection*

Chapter Eleven

The Pacers & Trotters

Racing horses with these special gaits — Pacing and Trotting — was truly an American development.

Flat racing and steeplechasing were sports for the more affluent.

The term trotting is used in a general way and means horses that either trotted or paced.

The sport was enjoyed by every one — a country road or a city park could be all the track needed for a short dash to prove the merits of your horse.

County Fairs and State Fairs had trotting racers as a standard event all during the last half of the nineteenth century and well into the twentieth century.

This type of racing became a national pastime.

Trotters and pacers as a breed are "Standardbreds" and are an all-around horse. They could be driven or ridden or worked.

When a horse paces, he moves his legs in lateral pairs, while a trotter moves his legs in diagonal pairs.

In this writing, there is not space to cover adequately the hundreds of magnificent horses that have made their marks in this great sporting event. So, we have picked on one horse to represent the sport, the legendary Dan Patch.

In 1905, he paced the mile in 1:55 ¼, a recognized record that stood for 33 years.

Dan Patch was the epitome of excellence in this sport. He broke the two-minute barrier 35 times in his pacing career.

This horse, a mahogany bay in color, was foaled in 1896. Four years later, he started serious racing. By 1902, competition was difficult to locate so his owner M.W. Savage began to race the fantastic speedster against the time clock.

Dan Patch became a national hero. Thousands of lithographs of his portrait were mailed on request.

Products were named after him. There were Dan Patch cigars, Dan Patch coaster wagons, rocking horses, sleds, watches, washing machines, sheet music and even a Dan Patch automobile that sold for $525.

Dan Patch died in 1916 of a heart ailment and the entire country mourned his passing.

To be let to Mares this Seaſon.

At Mr. Philip Platt's on Long-Iſland, Queen's County, and State of New-York, within about fifteen miles of the City of New-York, and within about three or four miles of the town of Jamaica, and in the neighbourhood of the Townſhip of Newton and Fluſhing,

At FIVE POUNDS the Seaſon for each Mare, the Money to be paid by firſt of September next.

Any Perſon wiſhing to bargain for a Sure Colt, will be treated with at the abovementioned place on reaſonable Terms, as he has proved himſelf a noted Sure Fold getter, where he has formerly ſtood, in New-Jerſey and Pennſylvania.

The Full Blooded Horſe

Meſsenger.

Imported in May, 1788.

MESSENGER is a Grey, full fifteen hands three inches high. He was bred by John Pratt, E . of New-Market, and was got by Membrino, who coverd at twenty-five guineas a mare, in 1784. Membrino wasgot by Engineer, who was got by Sampſon, who was the ſire of Bay Malton, and ſeveral other capital racers. His Dam by Turf ; his Grand-dam Regulus. This mare was ſiſter to Figerant, and was the dam of Leviathan, a capital racer

MESSENGER won the following Sums in the years1783, 1784, and 1785, as may be ſeen by the Racing Calendar

	Guineas.
In September, 1783, he beat at Newmarket Mr Power Colcheſter, by Shark,	100
Alſo Mr. Standly's Horse brother to Straightlegs,	30
October 30. 1783. he beat Mr. Napier's Horſe Spectre, acroſs the Flat,	300
And Mr. Fox's Horſe Pyrrhus, acroſs the New Flat,	150
May, 1784 he beat Lord Borringdon's Trigger	25
July, 1784. he beat Mr. Windham's Horſe Apothecary,	200
Lord Foley's Rodney, Mr. Weſtell's Snowdrop, and Mr.Clark's Flamer,	60
And Lord Foley's Ulyſſes,	100
March, 1785, he beat his Royal Highneſs the Prince of Wales Horſe Ulyſſes,	200
Alſo, Mr. Windham's Horſe Fortitude,	300
April, 1785, he beat Lord Sherborne's Horſe Taylor,	50
	1,515

N. B. In addition to the above, he has won the Kings Plate, and which is the only Horſe on the Conunent ſaid to have done the ſame.

Paſture to be had in the Neighbourhood on reaſonable Terms

THE FATHER OF THE TROTTING BREED

In 1788, the English Thoroughbred stallion Messenger was imported to America. He is considered to be the progenitor of the trotting horses in the U.S. This flyer was posted in the fall of that year offering the services of this stallion. Hambletonian 10, foaled in 1849, descends in a direct male line from Messenger. Dan Patch is a direct descendent from Hambletonian 10.

— Anna Fox Collection

A typical scene at all Fairs. The trotting races were big events. Mostly the horses entered were locally owned which added to the interest and excitement. Pictured here is a 1911 race at the Boonville, New York, Fair with the crowd packed around the finish line.

— *Ron Ryder Collection*

M.W. Savage and his great Dan Patch, 1:55 ¼. This photo of Dan's head was reproduced on a lithograph that was distributed by the thousands. The horse was a beautiful Mahogany Bay in color. He was purchased in 1902 by Mr. Savage for $60,000 and was stabled at a 750-acre farm 18 miles from Minneapolis.

— *Anna Fox Collection*

The Lexington, Kentucky, track. A true to form race with all the horses bunched together at the first turn.

— *Anna Fox Collection*

Dan Patch was called "The fastest harness horse the world has ever seen." His record included many world records and the horse was undefeated when this photo was taken in 1905.

— *Anna Fox Collection*

The Beautiful Solid Silver, Gold Lined Loving Cup Presented to Dan Patch on Christmas by the Kentucky Trotting Horse Breeders Association in Commemoration of Dan's Wonderful Mile in 1:55¼ at Lexington, Oct. 7, 1905.

This cup is 18 inches high, without the base, and one of the most beautiful of designs. Dan celebrated Christmas by eating apples out of this very beautiful and valuable present, which carried with it the best wishes of the great Kentucky Trotting Horse Association.

Dan Patch, even though he raced against the clock and not other horses, was a celebrity and drew enormous crowds to the fair grounds whenever he appeared. The photo is of his private railroad car.

— Anna Fox Collection

The caption of this photo read: A picture "of Dan's wonderful mile in 1:55 ¼ at Lexington, KY., October 7, 1905. The frontrunner is being driven by Scott Hudson, while Charley Dean is driving the outside runner. This picture was taken just before Dan Patch reached the wire at the finish of this great mile, and shows exactly how the pacemakers are used in stimulating Dan to his marvelous bursts of speed. Harry Hersey is driving Dan, who is flying through the air with every foot off the ground. This is the only good photograph ever taken of the finish of a world record mile, and is as life-like as if you stood on the track and saw the horses as they came dashing along in mighty efforts to beat Old Father Time."

— Anna Fox Collection

The strident sound of the ringing bell indicated that this San Fransisco fire house where Engine Company No. 2 is stationed, must respond. Probably as little as 10 to 12 seconds later, the three grays, with a clatter of hooves and clanging bell, are galloping up the street.

In this 1897 scene on Bush Street it is evident that the fireman has already ignited a handful of kerosene-soaked waste and has his fire under the boiler well started.

— *Wells Fargo Bank History Room*

Chapter Twelve

Answering the Fire Alarm

It is interesting, that as time goes by, there are those who buck improvements sometimes described as progress. This was true around 1850 when the volunteers who lugged fire fighting equipment over the streets answering an alarm, saw the handwriting on the wall when some departments began to use horses. No way could horses do a better job — but they did, thus the ladders were longer, chemical tanks larger and pumpers more powerful.

However, by the second decade of the twentieth century, the same old refrain was heard when motorized equipment became prevelant. Horses were more dependable and cheaper, the men said. Trucks, they were told, would do a better job — and they did, thus ladders were longer, chemical tanks larger and pumpers more powerful.

The last horse drawn piece of fire equipment used in Los Angeles was in 1922. The following year was the last year for Chicago and the next, for Troy, New York. Cities all across the country were following suit.

In their approximately 75 years of service, the fire department horses became an intelligent and integral part of the company to which they were assigned.

They learned the alarm signal that indicated their station. They were at attention when their stall doors flew open or the restraining chains dropped. They trotted out to their exact assigned position on a certain piece of equipment. They stood at attention while the swinging harnesses dropped on their bodies and were buckled in place. Within seconds of the sound of the alarm they were moving out of the station door into the daylight or dark of night, into pouring rain or sleet or snow or zero weather and galloping to the fire.

Generally the fire departments preferred four- to five-year-old geldings that weighed 1,500 to 1,600 pounds and were 16 to 17 hands. For smaller pieces of equipment, lighter horses were used, of course.

Because of the pounding over paved streets at a gallop, the horses' feet were vulnerable to damage. Even so, many horses were in the demanding fire service for 10 or more years.

The number of horses used in a fire department was determined by the size of the community which, in turn, decided the number of fire stations. In 1897, Chicago had 500 horses in service. A year later, Milwaukee had 160 horses in the fire department. Some departments were large enough to employ their own veterinarians, farriers and even wheelwrights.

After a fire the horses were walked up and down the street until they cooled off and were dry enough to be curried and brushed. If there were no alarms, the horses were exercised on a daily basis. The emphasis was always on the absolute best care possible for their valuable and well-trained animals.

Winter conditions in the northern cities always added to the problems. Some departments would add two horses ahead of a three-abreast on a heavy pumper. Other departments put some of the smaller rigs on sled runners. All departments added calks to the shoes of the horses.

The swinging harness was a great innovation that came along in 1871 in St. Joseph, Missouri. It eliminated the need to keep the horses harnessed all the time. If they were not harnessed, the swinging harness surely shortened the time between the alarm and departure from the station.

In this type of harness, no buckles were used — only large snap catches. The hames became part of the collar and were open at the bottom instead of the top. This unusual and very practical invention and its use spread rapidly. It soon became standard equipment and reduced the time between the incoming alarm and the horses moving out of the station to around 10 to 12 seconds.

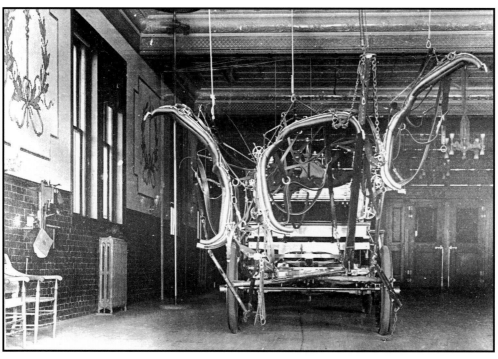

Left: The swinging harness in position ready to accept the three horses that will pull this piece of equipment. The horses are trained to trot from their stalls and position themselves in front of their assigned vehicle and in their exact position. Time was of the essence.

— *Carnegie Library of Pittsburgh*

Below: Inside a Boston Fire House at the turn of the century. A two-horse wagon stands ready.

— *Bill Noonan Collection*

Interior of a Lawrence, Massachusetss, fire house.
Firemen throughout the country, then and now, keep their
equipment station neat and clean — spic and span.

— *Bill Noonan Collection*

Responding to an alarm down Massachusetts Avenue in Boston, c. 1910. With the huge piece of six-ton equipment rumbling behind them and the fire bell clanging a warning, the horses gallop furiously down the street.

Note a hose wagon close behind.

— *Bill Noonan Collection*

The horses on this pumper seem to be flying over the pavement as they pull this heavy New York City, Engine Company No. 47, pumper.

— *Bill Noonan Collection*

Left: Boston Company E-28 around 1900. The steamer is located between guide rails on the floor to ensure it is placed in the exact same spot each time it is backed into the station. There is a connection with a hot water boiler in the basement that pumps hot water into the boiler on the steamer. Thus, at the time of an alarm, less time is required to produce steam to pump water.

— *Bill Noonan Collection*

Below: Engine Company No. 29 in Boston responding. The two horses out in front have been added for the winter to help power the heavy steamer through the snow-filled streets.

— *Bill Noonan Collection*

Left: Aerial Ladder Engine Company No. 12 in St. Paul, Minnesota. These ladder wagons were so long that the rear wheels were controlled by the tillerman. This enabled the long rig to get around corners.

— *Dr. H. J. McGinnis Collection*

Below: Minneapolis fire department four horse teams on their equipment. This rig is just swinging out of the fire station already at a full gallop.

— *Minnesota Historical Society*

The clanging bell and galloping horses pulling this long hook and ladder have stirred up enough excitement to get the kids on the sidewalk racing the horses. 1893, New Haven, Connecticut.

Note that one fireman is busy pulling on his rubber boots.

— *New Haven Colony Historical Society*

Left: Ladder Company No. 3 leaving the Bristol Street quarters in Boston. The horses are at almost a full gallop even before they are pulling the heavy load straightaway down the street.

— *Dr. H. J. McGinnis*

Below: Swinging around a corner at almost full speed is this Boston Chemical Company F. C. 1911.

— *Bill Noonan Collection*

Left: High pressure hose wagon in New York is a heavy enough load to require three horses. Note the roller wheel behind the team. A second such wheel is hidden behind the legs of the near horse. When this rig reaches the fire and the wagon is spotted, a pin will be pulled and the horses will be moved away from the action. The wagon poles will rest on these roller wheels.

— *Dr. H. J. McGinnis Collection*

Below: Engine Company No. 25 in Boston responding. Fire horses weighed between 1,200 and 1,400 pounds. They were quick on their feet and fast.

Heavy horses weighing 2,000 pounds were too clumsy and slow.

— *Bill Noonan Collection*

Kresge's Dime Store seems to be in bad shape. The Aerial Ladder truck stands stripped of its equipment. The aerial ladder itself is reaching to the fourth floor, it appears. The horses stand patiently waiting to return their assigned equipment to the fire house.

— *Philip Weber Collection*

Left: Fire Insurance Patrol Company responding to an alarm in Milwaukee.

— *Dr. H. J. McGinnis Collection*

Below: An East Boston fire, c. 1905. The horses have been blanketed to keep the raw wind off their sweated bodies while they wait.

— *Bill Noonan Collection*

A 1911 Milwaukee fire. Amid all the hubub and smoke, the fire horses stand unattended.

— *Milwaukee Public Museum*

The excitement, shouting and smoke does not perturb the fire horses. They are trained to tolerate the wait and stand quietly.

— *Bill Noonan Collection*

Left: After the fire, the big rig is about to be backed into the station. The team is swinging the long hook and ladder around to position it so it can be backed into the arched doorway. Boston, C. 1905.

— *Bill Noonan Collection*

Below: The firemen "heave-ho" on the mighty aerial ladder truck as they assist the three horses in getting the rig back into its Pittsburgh station house.

— *Carnegie Library, Pittsburgh*

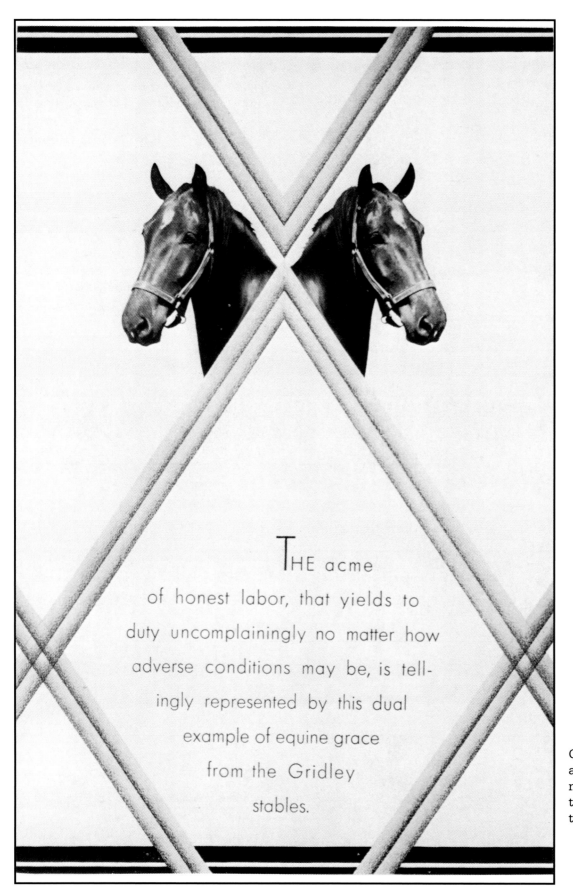

THE acme
of honest labor, that yields to
duty uncomplainingly no matter how
adverse conditions may be, is tell-
ingly represented by this dual
example of equine grace
from the Gridley
stables.

The Gridley Dairy Co. of Milwaukee advertising department produced this ad that complimented their loyal horses.

— *Author's Collection*

Chapter Thirteen

Promoting Products

Most major companies in the era of horse drawn wagons took great pride in their horses.

Quality was demanded because the company name appeared on the side of the delivery wagon. They wanted their horses to be well-fed, well-groomed, and well-shod — horses that would turn heads.

The horses in many cases were uniform in color. The H. J. Heinz Co. wagons were all white and they used black horses. Armour Packing Company used yellow wagons and dapple gray horses. Milk delivery wagons were generally white with dark colored horses.

These efforts are but a few examples of the strong desire of a company to promote and advertise their horse power.

Many of the big companies owned six- and eight-horse hitches that competed in the county or state fairs and frequently in the well-known shows such as the International in Chicago or Kansas City's Royal.

In this era everybody, it seemed, knew and loved to observe good horse flesh. This deep interest did not slip by the big corporations. They used these classy six- and eight-horse teams to promote both company and product.

These show teams were hand-picked horses to match in size, color, conformation and intelligence.

In 1910, Mr. Fred Pabst, President of Pabst Brewery in Milwaukee, said, referring to the sixes and eights: "They are great benefactors to the agriculture interests by influencing breeders to raise higher class stock."

Indeed, even today as this is written, Anheuser-Busch Company has three promotional hitches of Clydesdales on the road. Coors Brewery has a team of Belgians driven by Dick Sparrow. H. J. Heinz has a beautiful team of black Percherons on the road — and there are others.

Swift and Company sported six dapple gray Percherons in the early 1920s.

— Author's Collection

In 1931, when this photo was taken, the Carnation Company said their Champion team of eight Percherons averaged 2,185 pounds each.

— *Jim Richendollar Collection*

The $100,000 Internationally Famous, WILSON & CO, Six-Horse Matched Team of Clydesdales

In the 1920s and 1930s, Wilson Packing Company of Chicago showed their Clydesdales in many fairs and shows.

— *Author's Collection*

A 1904 photo of the Pabst Co. Brewing Co. Percheron team. The beautiful teams these big companies had were in great demand. They performed many maneuvers including a figure-eight at a smart trot. The brewers and packers, who were the primary exhibitors of these teams, spent thousands of dollars annually on printed material featuring their magnificent horses. The teams were a wonderful advertising medium.

— *Philip Weber Collection*

Anheuser-Busch's Clydesdales pulling a stake wagon.

— *Percheron Horse Association of America*

For many years, the Genesee Brewing Co. in Rochester, New York, promoted their product with this twelve-horse team of roan Belgians.

— Jim Richendollar Collection

National Biscuit Company's Clydesdale team.

— Jim Richendollar Collection

The Armour Greys

Probably the most incredible promotional stunt of all time involving a championship six-horse hitch was that agreed to between the Armour Packing Company of Chicago, and the Sells-Floto Circus, a big railroad show out of Denver.

Billboard magazine, in their March 20, 1909, issue, ran an announcement headlined "Armour Prize Team with Sells-Floto Shows." The story pointed out that in addition to the horses and wagon, all of the trophies, ribbons and other prizes which these remarkable animals have carried off will also be exhibited. The story stated that the horses will be dressed in their gold-trimmed harness in daily street parades and do wonderful stunts on the hippodrome at performances. Bill Wales, expert whip, has also been secured for the tour. The story concluded by stating "Unquestionably, the Armour greys are one of the biggest features that has been secured for a circus in late years."

Sells-Floto Circus, travelling on 30 railroad cars, opened in Denver March 29, 1909. The newspaper advertisements all mentioned "The $25,000 World Famous Prize Winners, the Armour Greys." The big show travelled south into New Mexico, to California, Oregon, Washington and into Canada, the Dakotas, and other upper midwest states, then east into Virginia, the Carolinas, south into Alabama and Mississippi,

where the show closed October 30, and returned to Denver.

Mostly all through this tour, the circus played one day stands. The Armour greys had plenty of exposure.

As the big circus toured Wisconsin, the newspapers always seemed to mention the Armour greys in their stories. The Chippewa Falls paper said "The famous Armour Greys were a great hit. The cups and prizes won by these renowned horses were on exhibition. Letters of admiration were displayed from King Edward of England and Emperor William of Germany."

The Superior paper commented "The famous Armour Greys $25,000 prize winning team driven by Billy Wales, the famous whip, who has driven this team at all the big horse shows of the world, was a big hit."

The Oshkosh paper said "The Armour & Co. team was admired everywhere along the route. The animals are closely matched and are aristocratic in appearance." In Kenosha, the comment was "The 11 o'clock parade was headed by the famous Armour team of greys which would be a feature for any show."

This 1909 tour was so successful that it was repeated for the 1910 circus season.

Above: The magnificent team of Percherons that were prize winners in America and Europe. In 1909 and 1910, the Armour Greys toured the U.S. with the Sells-Floto Circus parading in each city and performing daily in the matinee and evening performances.

—*Jim Richendollar Collection*

Left: Billy Wales, the sensational driver of the famous Armour team.

The Famed 20-Mule Team

Death Valley stretches across the state of California north of Los Angeles, and along the border with Nevada. It was in this dry, hot and desolate area that borax was discovered in 1881.

What began as a very practical development of transportation, the twenty-mule teams, ended up as one of America's best-known advertising trademarks.

Special wagons were built to haul the mined borax to the railroads some 160 miles away. To do the job efficiently, each train (two loaded wagons and a water tank wagon) had to haul 30 to 36 tons. This load required twenty mules.

In blistering temperatures of 136° to 150°, the mules moved the train 16 to 18 miles a day. A one-way trip took 10 days.

Ten of these enormous wagons were built at Mojave, California, at a cost of $900 each. Each wagon, when empty, weighed 7,800 lbs. and could carry about 12 1/2 tons of borax. The bodies were sixteen feet long, four feet wide and six feet deep. The axles were 3 1/2-inch square steel. The rear wheels were 7 feet in diameter and front wheels were 5 feet in diameter. The steel tires were 8 inches wide and one inch thick.

The tank wagon held 1,200 gallons of water for the men and mules.

Mules were used for this grueling work because of their reputation for endurance, sure-footedness, and their ability to stand up under the extreme heat.

The mules were driven on a jerk line with the skinner riding the near wheeler. In a downhill grade, he rode the box seat so he could manipulate the brake.

The team consisted of the wheelers, the pointers, the sixes and on out to the leaders.

The jerk line ran through rings on the harness of the near mules out to the leaders. A light iron rod called the jockey stick connected the leaders. One end was fastened to the chin strap of the off mule. The other end was fastened to a hame ring on the offside of the near leader.

A steady pull on the line and the call "haw" had the team turn left. A jerk on the line and the call "gee" turned them right.

The skinner had to know each mule. He was expected to be a practical vet in case of a sick animal. He also served as a farrier when a mule threw a shoe.

His assistant was called the swamper. The swamper's duty was to brake the second wagon when necessary. He helped in harnessing and unharnessing, feeding, and watering the team. The swamper was also the cook.

When the driver (skinner) needed to turn the train he could command the pointers and sixes over the chain. As the team started around a turn, the chain pulled into a straight line between the lead mule and the wagon. To keep the chain going around the curve, some of the spans of mules were called to hop over the chain and pull at an angle away from the curve. These spans would step along sideways until the corner had been turned, then the mules would hop back over the chain.

These teams operated from 1883 to 1889. It was in this period of time that the 20-mule team plodded into history. By 1896, the ingenious advertising people of the Pacific Coast Borax Company (predecessor of the United States Borax and Chemical Corporation) realized that the unique 20-mule team was a valuable symbol and they had it trademarked.

The trademark captured the imagination of the public and, ever since, has been promoted and used in advertisements. Today it is one of America's best known corporate slogans.

Over the years, U.S. Borax has maintained a set of wagons for promotional tours of the country, for ad photos and for television shows like "Death Valley Days" in the 1950s.

Left: The desolation and dryness of Death Valley through which the team traveled is evident in this photograph.

— *U.S. Borax Corporation*

Below: The Harmony Borax Works at about 1888. The mule team is about to start on its 160-mile trek.

— *U.S. Borax Corporation*

Teams being watered — an important chore on any farm.

— *J.C. Allen & Son*

Chapter Fourteen

In Agriculture

With the signing of the Armistice on Nov. 11, 1918, World War I came to a merciful end. In a way, this event in far off France marked the beginning of the end of the era when draft horses provided the power to till the soil and accomplish other farm chores.

This momentous event freed America's tractor, truck and auto manufacturers to concentrate on improving and selling their products for domestic consumption. Programs were also accelerated to improve the nation's roads and highways.

In January, 1919, the Army announced their first auction to sell off their surplus of almost 45,000 horses and mules in the U.S. They also had substantial surpluses in Europe. This prompted the Ohio Percheron Breeders Association to ask the Army not to return any animals from France because of a chance of spreading diseases in the U.S. Because of poor stabling facilities, inadequate feed, and a shortage of veterinarians, there were numerous horse diseases in wartime France.

The *Breeder's Gazette*, which claimed to be the "Farmer's Greatest Paper," kept publishing editorials, articles and letters from farmers around the country for the next two or three years that indicated the relentless trend away from draft horses on the farm.

Those who loved their horses did not want to give them up. In part, here is an editorial from the *Gazette* of March 13, 1919:

"A good horseman is a good farmer. The man who is devoted to his horses is careful of all other stock. He feels an interest in living things. A mind in sympathy with life processes in their various forms, finding enjoyment in the thrift of stock is the mind to grasp the full scope of farm production.

"On the other hand, the man who finds chief delight in tinkering with machinery misses the sympathetic viewpoint of one who prefers to fuss with livestock."

In the April 10, 1919, issue, the *Gazette* quoted a farmer as saying "The problem of service is a serious one. After all, the tractor is a complicated and somewhat delicate piece of mechanism. It has many ailments."

A Minnesota farmer put in his ideas: "It is only a question of time when the horse will come back to its own and prove its value compared with the tractor. At the present time, the enormous amount of advertising done by the tractor manufacturers has led farmers to believe that it is economical to buy tractors.

"This condition brings to memory the situation 35 years ago when tractor (steam) manufacturers put out some good advertising and sold to practically every fourth farmer. Only one out of ten of the tractors purchased then made good and it is only about one out of ten bought now which will prove a profitable investment."

Then in October, an Illinois farmer wrote "I heard from three farmers. All agree that the tractor has become a necessity upon the huge farms. All three state it supplements but does not replace the horses."

A month later, in the Nov. 20, 1919, issue, the *Breeder's Gazette* editorialized "Public ignorance is the principal enemy of the horse in America.

In the Nov. 13 issue we heard from Wayne Dinsmore, Secretary of the Percheron Society of America, in a major article. Here are a few excerpts:

"If they (horses) are to continue to hold a place in the world, it must be because they have certain advantages over other types of motive power.

"The great flexibility of power in horses is especially valuable on the farm. One eight-horse team on a double disc with a harrow behind may later be broken into two four-horse teams for seeding or into one pair for planting, a four for harrowing, and an extra pair for general work. No other source of power in actual use on the farm has this flexibility.

"Production of horses has a definite influence on family life on the farm. The use of horses as power units interests the farmer and family in the production of other good livestock and stock production inculcates in children a liking for the land. No such training comes about where other types of motive power are used. On the contrary, the training required along mechanical lines leads a great many youngsters into factory work where they are lost to the farm for all time. Farm life is favorable to clear thinking and right living. Farm children develop into clear-cut, clean-minded youths who are the bulwark of the nation."

Three weeks later, an Illinois farmer wrote a strong rebuttal to Mr. Dinsmore. "He (Dinsmore) says the more tractors are bought, the more must be built, the more iron and more coal mined, and the more smelters and steel mills operated, all of which call for more men from the farms. Are not the mines, smelters and factories keeping pace with the farmer in adaptation and use of labor-saving machinery? After all, who would like to turn the wheels of progress backward and reverse the order of things?

"Only when we have our farms run by skilled and scientific farmers who are also skilled mechanics using labor-saving machinery, thereby making the farmer independent of farm laborers, will we approach ideal conditions."

In a December 1919 issue, an article in the *Gazette* stated that in 1916, there were 35,000 tractors on farms. In 1917, 50,000 were purchased and in 1918, 100,000 were purchased. In 1919, an estimated 200,000 to 250,000 tractors were in actual use on farms.

"A continued increase would soon place a tractor on nearly every farm. This fact gives the horse interests grounds for worry.

"The first tractors were almost universally unsatisfactory. Those purchased in the last three or four years are giving much better service.

"Why are farmers who buy tractors not able to dispose of a larger proportion of their horses? The answer is that tractors in their present form and design are not adaptable to nearly all farm work for which tractive power is needed. A man must keep enough horses to do the work which cannot be done satisfactorily with the tractor.

In the Feb. 12, 1920, issue, a Wisconsin farmer piped up and said "It seems to me that most are missing an important point. In almost every instance, tractors were purchased primarily for belt work, silo fillers, huskers and threshers."

In May 1920, a *Gazette* article said "Horses are coming back. Farmers sold off good horses too soon. They also stopped breeding mares."

A Washington farmer wrote "As a general thing, their (horses') days of usefulness as a needed power plant are over and the sooner the horse raiser heeds the sign of the times, the better off he will be."

A Minnesota farmer disagreed. "I hold that good draft horses are and always will be the best and most economical power on the farm. The life of a tractor is not more than eight years. Horses have worked 15 years without repairs.

"Horses are dependable power. Their spark plugs do not get dirty. The wiring never goes wrong, the radiator never leaks, the water does not freeze nor does the carburetor clog. With a tractor, one has all these things to contend with."

In June, 1920, a Wyoming farmer commented "An auto expert is quoted in the *Denver Post* as saying that the horse as a power unit on the American farm was dying hard, but surely. If this expert could have seen our roads blocked with snow, with tractors standing in the sheds and horses hauling hay to cattle that would have starved, he would have another statement to make.

"There have been millions of cars and trucks pulled out of snow drifts and mud holes by horses but show me the tractor or truck that ever pulled a horse out of a place he could not get through."

By the last half of 1920, the *Breeder's Gazette* was publishing articles and letters from farmers that pointed out the economies of tractors and trucks on the farm. One farmer wrote "I am not a horse-knocker but horses should be used to supplement tractors."

In just one issue, Feb. 21, 1921, the *Breeder's Gazette* had a photo of 25 farm boys who took a tractor short course at the School of Agriculture at Purdue University; a photo and story of a young farmer who purchased a truck and did hauling for neighbors to and from town and stockyards; a photo of a huge truckload of baled hay which was being unloaded into a barn loft; a photo of a truck with a manure spreader built onto the chassis.

Reading this great livestock journal over these years, one gets a reluctant feeling of them "throwing in the towel." Their editorial in the Feb. 17, 1921, issue was titled "The Handwriting on the Wall." They talked about heavy horses being scarce, foal crops below normal, and mares not bred. The editorial ends "The *Gazette* is neither boosting horses nor knocking automotive power for agricultural uses. Economic, efficient power, on four feet or on wheels, should be the primary object of both horse breeders and manufacturers of machinery."

A tractor hitch attached to a horse-drawn plow.

From Horses to Tractors

Just by observing the advertisements in the *Breeder's Gazette,* the premier livestock journal, a person could see the handwriting on the wall.

Like an outpouring of molten lava inexorably flowing down from the volcano, the manufacturers of tractors, trucks and autos were slowly and surely worming their products onto the farms of America.

In 1900, an issue might contain two pages of ads placed by horse and mule breeders, dealers and importers. There would be an occasional ad for a steam tractor or the Kelly-Springfield Tire Co. — but the ad was for hard rubber tires for carriages and buggies.

By 1915, there were many ads, 1/4 page, full page, and even two page spreads for GMC trucks, six or eight different autos, and many accessories such as oil, tires, spark plugs and tire chains. Usually, there continued to be two, or perhaps three, pages of ads for horses and mules.

Five years later, with World War I only a memory, the advertising campaign broke loose. Now the competition began to appear and the ads were usually 3/4 page or full page size.

The great array of tractors included the Samson, E-B Avery, IHC, Cleveland, Moline and Caterpillar. Trucks were pushed hard and included GM, White, Stoughton, Federal, Republic, Garford, Diamond T, Patriot, Packard and Maxwell.

At least a dozen automobiles were advertised as well as many accessories such as tires, motor oil, storage batteries, Timken axles, brake linings, spark plugs, tire chains and a carbon remover which was advertised as an engine laxative.

During this transition period, the ads for draft horses and mules hung in there — two full pages advertising the availability from breeders, dealers and importers.

One die-hard farmer wrote "As long as we see the footprints of man, we will see the footprints of the horse. The horse is second nature to man."

As we look around today, 70 years later, to a degree we must admit this farmer was right in his prediction.

When draft horses did all the work, one of the advantages was that the farmer could raise his own replacement power. The disadvantage was it took about 30 acres to raise feed and another 30 acres for pasture. This varied, of course, depending on the number of horses a farmer owned.

— *J.C. Allen & Son*

Three powerful blacks pull a one-bottom plow.

— *Philip Weber Collection*

Left: One of the chores was spreading manure from the stable, cow barn and pig sty.

— *Percheron Horse Association of America*

Below: Spring tooth harrow breaks up the soil prior to planting.

— *Author's Collection*

Six Percherons pull a two-bottom plow and harrow.

— *Author's Collection*

Left: A beautiful team of roan Belgians bring a load of hay to the barn.

— *Philip Weber Collection*

Below: Stacking hay.

— *Percheron Horse Association of America*

Left: Spring corn planting is handled easily by this team.

— *Author's Collection*

Below: Hay is turned for curing and windrowed for easy loading.

— *J.C. Allen & Son*

The horses on these oat binders are protected from flies with lightweight nets that cover their bodies and heads.

— *Philip Weber Collection*

Threshing wheat on an Iowa farm. The men in the center are bagging the wheat.

— *Milwaukee Public Museum*

Thirty-three horses are at work pulling this harvester in 1902 at Walla Walla, Washington. In that period of time, the U.S. produced 756 million bushels of wheat a year, 26 percent of the world's crop. Prices ranged from 61¢ to 95¢ per bushel.

This enormous harvester includes a header, thresher, seperator, fanning mill and sacker. This rig will cut from 60 to 125 acres a day and thresh 1,700 to 3,000 bushels a day.

— *Robert J. Chandler*
Collection

Threshing wheat. A load of shocks is being tossed into the machine. The straw is stacked and the wheat is bagged then loaded into a waiting wagon.

— *Milwaukee Public Museum*

Four teams provide the power to operate this corn sheller in Nebraska.

Below: Farmers brought their milk to town to the processing factory. In this scene at Constableville, New York, 40-gallon cans are being used.

— *Ron Ryder Collection*

Wagon No. 5, heavily-loaded with dining department equipment, heads for the lot with an eight-horse hitch.

— *Circus World Museum, Baraboo, Wis.*

Chapter Fifteen

Circus Comes to Town

In 1872, P. T. Barnum started his circus moving from town to town on railroad flat cars, rather than having horses pull the wagons overland. During that decade just about every major circus became a railroad show. That did not mean that the circuses did not use as many horses — just the opposite.

The wagons were larger and the shows got bigger which meant more wagons, thus more horses. For example, the biggest of them all was Ringling Bros. and Barnum & Bailey Combined Shows. In the 1920s and 1930s, they required 90 to 100 railroad cars to move the show. They carried 300 to 350 grade Percherons plus perhaps 300 performing horses.

These were the days of one day stands. In July of 1928, for instance, the Ringling Circus left Chicago on the 22nd, played Milwaukee the 23rd, then on through Wisconsin — Sheboygan on the 24th, Oshkosh the 25th, Green Bay the 26th, Wausau the 27th, Eau Claire the 28th, then Madison and south into Illinois towns.

When the big trains with their silver cars loaded with red wagons rolled into town early in the morning, the railroad crossing area where the show would unload was generally packed with people waiting for the action.

The big draft horse teams were first to appear from the special stock cars as they were needed immediately to unload wagons. This was the first of the free shows on circus day.

Hauling this train load of colorful and exciting equipment from the railroad yards over city streets a mile, sometimes two miles or more, to the showgrounds using teams of six or eight Percherons was free show number two.

At the showgrounds, these big teams arrived with the heavy red wagons. The tents were erected and the showgrounds were made ready for the afternoon show — free show number three.

When all the above was up and ready, it was time for the street parade. Canvas covers were removed from the beautiful gold and silver and red bandwagons and tableaux, sides of the cages were removed to reveal the exotic animals, flags were flying, equestrians in wardrobe, all the draft horses with 18-inch bridle feather plumes, bands on some wagons, steam calliope ready, camels and elephants lined up — down through the town's streets to the business district. This was free show number four. The horse drawn parade was an advertisement; it let people know today was circus day. It stirred up their excitement. It brought the townspeople out to the showgrounds. The show in the big tent was not free — a ticket would cost 25¢ or 50¢ or maybe 75¢, depending on the era and size of the circus.

After the evening performance, everything in sight on the showgrounds was packed into wagons. The big teams hauled them all back to the railroad yards where they were loaded onto the waiting train. This was free show number five, that is if you were not too worn out watching all the activity. When everything and everybody was loaded, the blast of the locomotive whistle was heard and the circus train slipped off into the dark of night headed for the next town 100 miles away.

Everyone who admired good horse flesh had a very satisfying day.

The draft horse era of the big railroad circuses came to a close in the late 1930s.

Above: As soon as the 72-foot long stock cars were spotted, the baggage stock was unloaded. They were put together as a six or an eight. This photo shows Ringling Bros. and Barnum & Bailey Circus in the 1920s.

— *Circus World Museum,*
Baraboo, Wisconsin

Left: Once the wagons are unloaded, they were hauled to the showgrounds. Generally, each team made two trips in morning and two at night.

— *Author's Photo*

Left: Eight blue roans pull the heavily-loaded stringer wagon which was 20- to 25-feet long. They are enroute to the showgrounds. Note all the body poles are dragging on the ground indicating the wheel team is doing all the work. Circuses used long neck chains so the weight of the body poles was not on the horses.

— *Gordon Carver Photo*

Below: A pull over team moves a wagon across the flat cars. The man leaning over the wagon pole is steering it. He was called a poler.

— *Gene Baxter Collection*

There are probably 32 horses on this Ringling Bros. pole wagon. The circus can't wait for the sun to come out from behind the clouds to dry off the lot because tomorrow's town is already heavily billed as are the next 14 dates.

— *Steve Albasing Photo*

On occasions, because of some problem on the railroad, the circus would arrive late in town. When this occurred, the horse tops (tents) were not erected and all the stock was tied to picket lines as seems to be the case in this 1922 photograph of Ringling Bros. and Barnum and Bailey Circus.

— *Author's Collection*

The body poles are all off the ground indicating all eight horses are sharing this heavy load on the Hagenbeck - Wallace Circus.

— *Dick Hemphill Collection*

On June 30, 1917, when Ringling Bros. Circus arrived at the assigned showgrounds in Niagra Falls, New York, it was a sea of mud. There appears to be a six horse team hitched to the wagon but they could not handle the load under these rough conditions. Hook rope teams were called in. The eight on the far right and the six grays in the center hook on to large steel rings on the wagon side. The blacks on the left side are most likely hooked to the gooseneck on the wagon pole. With 26 or 28 horses, the wagon was spotted where it was needed.

— *Steve Albasing Photo*

Left: The big shows carried their own canvas watering troughs.

— *Gene Baxter Collection*

An early morning scene June 21, 1909, in Milwaukee. Barnum & Bailey Circus was in town for two shows that day. The big wagons are beginning to arrive at the showgrounds from the railroad unloading area. Townspeople swarm over the lot to watch the exciting free show of putting up the tents. See photo bottom of next page.

— *Milwaukee Public Museum*

The wheels of heavily loaded wagon No. 55 are sinking into the soft lot. Two hook rope teams are assisting the eight-horse team on the wagon. 1930 in New Orleans. Ringling Bros. and Barnum & Bailey Circus.

— *Dick Hemphill Collection*

About three hours later, the huge 10-acre lot is transformed into a canvas city. Predominate in the background behind the tree is the big top where the performances will be given in front of perhaps 10,000 people each show. Way off to the left in the distant haze is the menagerie tent. The tent on the left is the dressing room. The next day, June 22, this lot will be empty but all the tents will be in place in Tomah, Wisconsin, 162 miles northwest of Milwaukee for two shows in that town.

— *Milwaukee Public Museum*

Part of a day's work for the draft stock is the street parade through the business district. Here, the Forepaugh - Sells Bros. Circus No. 1 bandwagon with its team of 10 Percherons parade through Baraboo, Wisconsin in 1911.

— *Author's Collection*

Left: Eighteen-inch feather plumes on the bridles of the draft horses are standard equipment for dressing up the street parade. Note the body poles dragging on the pavement. The long neck chains allow this which was standard procedure on circuses.

— *Author's Collection*

Below: The other four or six horses of this long string are probably tethered to the opposite side of the pole wagon. When the team's work is done, they will be taken to the horse tents where they will be unharnessed, groomed, watered, fed and allowed to rest until late in the afternoon.

— *Author's Collection*

On August 30, 1918, the Barnum & Bailey Circus paraded through the downtown streets of Tacoma, Washington. Signs on two of the wagons plugged purchasing war stamps.

— *Paul Wissler Collection*

Index

Index

Index